3·50

General editor: Graham Handley MA Ph.D.

B

J
Fo

First published 1991 by
Pan Books Ltd, Cavaye Place, London SW10 9PG

9 8 7 6 5 4 3 2 1

© Pan Books Ltd 1991

ISBN 0 330 50331 6

Photoset by Parker Typesetting Service, Leicester

Printed in England by Clays Ltd, St Ives plc

Contents

Preface by the general editor vi

The dramatic background 1

The author and his work 3

The Birthday Party 5

Act commentaries with textual notes and revision questions 7

Pinter's art in *The Birthday Party* 26

Characters 26
Stanley 26, Meg 28, Petey 29, Lulu 31, Goldberg 31, McCann 33

Themes 36
The Outsider 36; Violence and power 37; Women, men and sexuality 38; Memories, truth and illusion 39

Language and comedy 40

Structure 42

General questions on *The Birthday Party*, with a sample answer in note form 44

The Caretaker 47

Act commentaries with textual notes and revision questions 49

Pinter's art in *The Caretaker* 65

Characters 65
Davies 65, Mick 68, Aston 69

Themes 72
Violence and menace/the Outsider 72; Power 73; Failure to communicate 74; Loneliness and betrayal 75; Other themes 76

Setting and structure 78

Language 80

General questions on *The Caretaker*, with a sample answer in note form   81

The Homecoming   83

Act commentaries with textual notes and revision questions   85

Pinter's art in *The Homecoming*   103

Characters   103
Ruth 103, Teddy 105, Lenny 106, Max 108, Joey 110, Sam 110

Themes   112
The Outsider 112; Women and sexuality 113; Power and survival 114; Memories, truth and illusion 115

Language and comedy   117

Structure   119

General questions on *The Homecoming*, with a sample answer in note form   120

Further reading list   122

Page references in this Note are to the Eyre Methuen editions of the three plays in Methuen's Modern Plays series. As references are given to individual Acts it can, however, be used with any edition of the plays.

Preface by the general editor

The intention throughout this study aid is to stimulate and guide, to encourage your involvement in the book, and to develop informed responses and a sure understanding of the main details.

Brodie's Notes provide a clear outline of the play or novel's plot, followed by act, scene, or chapter summaries and/or commentaries. These are designed to emphasize the most important literary and factual details. Poems, stories or non-fiction texts combine brief summary with critical commentary on individual aspects or common features of the genre being examined. Textual notes define what is difficult or obscure and emphasize literary qualities. Revision questions are set at appropriate points to test your ability to appreciate the prescribed book and to write accurately and relevantly about it.

In addition, each of these Notes includes a critical appreciation of the author's art. This covers such major elements as characterization, style, structure, setting and themes. Poems are examined technically – rhyme, rhythm, for instance. In fact, any important aspect of the prescribed work will be evaluated. The aim is to send you back to the text you are studying.

Each study aid concludes with a series of general questions which require a detailed knowledge of the book: some of these questions may invite comparison with other books, some will be suitable for coursework exercises, and some could be adapted to work you are doing on another book or books. Each study aid has been adapted to meet the needs of the current examination requirements. They provide a basic, individual and imaginative response to the work being studied, and it is hoped that they will stimulate you to acquire disciplined reading habits and critical fluency.

Graham Handley 1991

The dramatic background

In the mid-1950s, the drama critic Kenneth Tynan wrote dismissively of the typical West End play of the time:

Its setting is a country house in what used to be called Loamshire but is now, as a heroic tribute to realism, called Berkshire . . . The inhabitants belong to a social class partly derived from romantic novels and partly from the playwright's view of the leisured life he will lead after the play is a success.

However, even as Tynan wrote, drama of this cosy, reassuring type was already a spent force, yielding to more experimental plays by 'New Wave' writers like John Osborne, Arnold Wesker and John Arden. Osborne's *Look Back in Anger* (1956), Wesker's *Chicken Soup with Barley* (1958) and Arden's *Serjeant Musgrave's Dance* (1959) brought a biting political and social dimension to drama which had been missing hitherto. Instead of offering escapism from the routine of life, plays like these challenged the preconceptions of the audience; their function was to question, provoke and disturb. In *Look Back in Anger*, for instance, Osborne created in Jimmy Porter a character who epitomized the hostility of British youth toward the stuffy, class-ridden values which prevailed.

Like all such terms, though, 'New Wave' can be misleading if one thinks of a homogeneous group of writers sharing values, social attitudes and beliefs in what drama should be doing. For instance, although Pinter himself was seen as a 'New Wave' writer, his plays have nothing in common with those of Arden or Osborne. In *The Birthday Party*, *The Caretaker* and *The Homecoming* he shows little direct concern with political ideology or society at large. Instead, he presents individuals caught in the net of life. But what the 'New Wave' offered in their different ways was a radical reappraisal of what drama could offer.

Pinter's work has much in common with Samuel Beckett, whose most famous play, *Waiting for Godot* (1953), provoked puzzlement among audiences used to plays having a beginning, a middle and an end. Instead, they were presented with two tramps, Vladimir and Estragon, who are waiting for Godot. We are not told who Godot is, if he ever comes, or why they are waiting for him. Very little happens in terms of action: to pass the time, the tramps talk, often repeating what they have recently said; there are many occasions when they say nothing at all. When there is action, it is likely to be ineffective, obscure in its meaning or inconsequential in any contribution it makes to the plot development.

Even from this brief outline, we can see similarities between Pinter and Beckett. When we try to analyse what their plays are 'about', we run into difficulties. We are presented with situations which are at once simple and ambiguous and puzzling. What happens seems to be symbolic (that is, it suggests something larger and more significant than itself), but what it symbolizes is difficult to determine with any degree of precision.

In other words, Pinter, like Beckett, denies us the comfort of knowing what his plays 'mean'. The products of a post-war culture in which so much of life has lost any larger meaning, his plays refuse to offer us the consolation of an escapist world in which right always prevails and where, with the helpful guidance of the writer, we always know where we stand. Instead, we are left to make the best of it. Naturally we bring to these plays our own interpretations because as thinking human beings we are driven to impose some order and meaning on the world around us. But we are always uneasily aware that these interpretations are based upon the often unreliable information we have gleaned from what unreliable characters such as Goldberg, Davies or Lenny have said about themselves or others.

However, Pinter is no mere disciple of Beckett. His plays have their own distinctive 'voice' and method. Three examples will serve to show this: first, Pinter's characters and situations, although strange at first sight, are more psychologically realistic than Beckett's are; secondly, he is more concerned than Beckett is to show that menace exists even in the most domestic of contexts; thirdly, he is less concerned with abstract philosophical issues than Beckett is.

The author and his work

Pinter has said of *The Birthday Party* that menace does not come 'from extraordinary, sinister people, but from you and me; it is all a matter of circumstances'. This remark gives not only a helpful insight into the nature of Pinter's work but shows how the experiences of his early life might have influenced his writing. He was born into a Jewish family in 1930 in the East End of London (an area with a high immigrant population), the son of a tailor. Although his home life was reasonably comfortable, the growth of Fascism in the 1930s (with its hatred of Jews) and economic depression meant that during his early life he was made aware of insecurity and the threat of violence – for example, the British Fascists led by Sir Oswald Mosley organized marches only a few miles from where Pinter lived. This is not to say, of course, that there is a direct correlation between his life and his plays, but equally the circumstances of his youth must have made him aware of the insecurity, fear and smouldering resentment in which many seemingly ordinary people live.

He was educated at Hackney Downs Grammar School, proceeding from there in 1947 to the Royal Academy of Dramatic Art (RADA). He left after two terms. A year later, he was called up to do his National Service, refused to do so because he was a pacifist, went to a different drama school (Central School of Speech and Drama) in 1951 and then became an actor, adopting the stage name David Baron.

For several years he toured the country playing in repertory companies, learning the stagecraft which he has put to such good effect in his plays. His years as an actor, with their insecurity, rootlessness and experience of cheap lodging-houses, also reinforced the mood of uncertainty, of the fear just below the surface, which is typical of so much of his work.

It was not until 1957 that he first tasted success as a playwright when he agreed to write a play for a friend who was studying drama at Bristol University. Entitled *The Room*, Pinter wrote it in four days while acting in Devon. It came to the attention of Harold Hobhouse, influential drama critic of *The Times*, who reviewed it favourably. On the strength of this, Michael Codron, a producer, asked to see more of his work. *The Birthday Party*

3

(1958), *A Night Out* and *The Caretaker* (1959), *Night School* (1960), and *The Homecoming* (1964) were only some of the plays which followed in quick succession. Reviewers and audiences were not at first enthusiastic – *The Birthday Party* ran for six nights only in London – but critical acclaim soon followed and in 1966 Pinter was awarded the CBE.

As well as being one of the most influential and successful post-war playwrights, Pinter has also written some excellent film scripts, among them *The Go-Between* (1969, from L. P. Hartley's novel), *The Last Tycoon* (1974, from Scott Fitzgerald's novel), and *The French Lieutenant's Woman* (1981, from John Fowles' novel). In addition to his writing, he has acted in and directed his own work as well as that of other writers.

The Birthday Party

Act commentaries with textual notes and revision questions

Act One

Pages 9–13

The emptiness of the relationship between Meg and Petey is evident from the start of the play. Bound together by habit and custom, their conversation in their seaside boarding house is banal and incapable of any development. She asks him the most obvious and sometimes idiotic questions and he patiently replies while he eats the breakfast she takes great pride in having prepared, but which is, in fact, unappetizing. Pinter pushes the emptiness of their conversation to its very limits, with some of Meg's remarks casting doubts on her intelligence. Specially noteworthy here is the way he gives the impression of realistic conversation by emphasizing the way Meg, especially, repeats herself and states the obvious. For instance, when she asks Petey if he is back, she is actually looking at him through the hatch. What Pinter is illustrating here is not only that much conversation is pointless, but also that it only takes place to fill a silence most of us find too awkward to bear. Although little is happening in terms of dramatic action, these opening pages are crucial in the way they establish the relationship between Meg and Petey. They also present that ambiguity of tone which is such a mark of Pinter's writing. Meg and Petey are at once comic and pathetic; we find ourselves torn between wanting to laugh *at* and sympathize *with* them.

Petey's remark that two men have asked for accommodation adds another dimension to their conversation, that of Meg as proud landlady. She boasts of running a very good boarding house, even though the breakfast she has just given Petey suggests otherwise. This section closes with her determination to wake Stanley. To judge by the way she speaks of Stanley – he is a lazy boy whom she loves and she is proud of the way he plays the piano – we might be excused for thinking that Stanley is very young. When we discover him to be a man in his late thirties, we are taken aback at first; then we realize that Meg treats him as the son she never had, and smothers him with love and attention.

wears glasses A sign in Pinter of someone who is inadequate.
They're refreshing. It says so. A good example of Meg's gullibility.
 Throughout the play she believes what she is told.

Pages 13–24

The wild laughter from Meg when she wakes Stanley contrasts
with the passive, mild nature we have seen so far. The implication here is that Stanley awakens feelings in Meg which lie
dormant in her relationship with Petey. When Stanley actually
appears, Meg's treatment of him as though he were a child
becomes all the more incongruous. Unlike Petey, who is always
polite to Meg, Stanley is rude, demanding and critical; he
behaves like the spoiled child Meg thinks he is. His threat to
move to one of the smart hotels on the front hurts Meg's pride
and she quickly fetches him his fried bread. Throughout this
section, we notice that the basic pattern of her dialogue with her
husband is repeated with Stanley, but Stanley's response is very
different from Petey's. For Stanley is secure in the knowledge
that, although the motherly Meg might reprimand him, she will
never reject him, and this gives him the freedom to enjoy being
rude to her.

After Petey returns to work, Stanley once more taunts Meg.
When he sarcastically describes the fried bread as succulent,
Meg seems to misunderstand the meaning of the word, inter-
preting it as having a sexually suggestive connotation. Unable to
leave him alone, she ruffles his hair, provoking him to call her a
succulent old washing bag. She totally misses his sarcastic tone
here, and asks shyly, as though flattered, if she is really succulent. Here, Pinter introduces another strand into their relationship: latent sexuality. Later she strokes his arm sensually,
speaks of lovely afternoons she has had in Stanley's room, and
tickles the back of his neck in a flirtatious manner. Stanley
evokes both maternal and sexual responses from Meg.

Stanley provokes Meg by criticizing her as a bad wife, little
knowing that later in the play he is to be subjected to much more
effective and ruthless criticism by McCann and Goldberg. When
Meg mentions the two gentlemen who are coming to stay, Stanley's response is at first disbelieving, but then he becomes agi-
tated, trying to convince himself that they will not come. Why
the arrival of visitors should provoke such a response is not

explained; it is part of Pinter's creation of a mood of menace and anxiety through suggestion rather than precise explanation. The disruptive influence of outsiders upon the safety offered by a room is a recurring Pinter theme.

At a simple level, Stanley's response here could be anxiety that the presence of other visitors will necessarily mean Meg having less time to devote to him. However, he quickly reasserts himself, demanding tea and criticizing the familiar way Meg talks to him, and then, as if the effort is too great, groans and falls forward over the table. A little later, he boasts to Meg that he has the prospect of a job playing the piano in European nightclubs. This seems highly unlikely, as does his boast of the concert he gave at Lower Edmonton. As with other characters, Goldberg in particular, Pinter creates an aura of mystery and uncertainty about Stanley's past. He might actually believe what he is saying or he might be inventing a past in order to impress Meg.

Meg is quietly alarmed at the possibility of losing Stanley and pleads with him to stay. Stanley responds with a calculated but obscure piece of cruelty concerning men arriving in a van containing a wheelbarrow and looking for Meg. To us, the image is banal, but Meg becomes frightened. Pinter does not clarify for us the reason for Meg's terror, but what is strongly communicated is that beneath her placid surface run strong but obscure desires and fears. Stanley's cruelty is interrupted by the arrival of Lulu.

You deserve the strap i.e. you deserve to be beaten; another example of Meg's treating Stanley like the naughty child she never had.

Someone's taking the Michael. Someone is misleading you.

Lower Edmonton An area of north London. It contrasts markedly with the large European cities Stanley boasts of visiting like Berlin and Constantinople in that it lacks any foreign glamour. Pinter is mocking Stanley by having him boast that he gave a very important concert in what is in fact an ordinary location.

They came up to me . . . They carved me up To carve someone up means to humiliate or ridicule. We never know who 'they' are; as in many other Pinter plays, the word is used to indicate vaguely understood representatives of power and authority.

Did you pay a visit this morning? Have you been to the lavatory? It is the kind of question an over-anxious mother might ask a small child.

Pages 24–27

Meg has a whispered conversation with Lulu, who is a young, flirtatious girl in her early twenties. Stanley overhears. Meg leaves to go shopping and Lulu deposits a large parcel on the sideboard. This action in itself, together with her warning to Stanley not to touch it, arouses our interest in what it contains. The conversation Stanley and Lulu have is dramatically important because it reveals, by his need to boast to her, how insecure he is. As if to compensate for this, he decisively asks her to go away with him, but when questioned more closely speaks what borders on nonsense. Although he wants to go, he says, there is in fact nowhere to go, but he does not want to stay where he is. This at once shows his confusion, his inability to act with any purpose and his perpetual dissatisfaction.

Pages 27–33

When McCann and Goldberg, Meg's two visitors, enter, Stanley leaves through the back door without being seen. Pinter quickly establishes Goldberg as the dominant figure, urging McCann to relax, and speaking with glib assurance of happy days out he enjoyed with his Uncle Barney. His comments on culture and what it is to be a gentleman contrast oddly with the down-at-heel boarding house he and McCann are visiting. His manner, too, self-satisfied and self-assured, contrasts with McCann's anxiety. As we try to come to terms with who they are and why they have come to Meg's boarding house, a hint of menace is introduced when Goldberg speaks of the job they are on. This contrasts with his earlier remark that he has brought McCann away for a few days by the seaside. Pinter has already established Goldberg as a formidably smooth user of conventional, reassuring images, while at the same time suggesting the ruthlessness which exists below the surface. Alongside the menace, however, there is comedy, as, for instance, when McCann compliments Goldberg (a Jew) on being a true Christian, and when Goldberg speaks of their job in fluent, official tones unlikely to be fully understood by McCann.

Pinter's choice of a Jew and an Irishman as two of his central characters is important, not least because it shows his talent for adapting models from a wide range of theatrical experience for his own purpose. When he wrote the play, the Jews and Irish were often the butt of music hall jokes. By a clever twist, he makes Goldberg and McCann into a double act of the kind popular in comedy, and gives them a sinister edge. Instead of their being only the victims of ridicule as they are in the world of comedy, in *The Birthday Party* they are also the comic/threatening protagonists.

When Meg returns from shopping, Goldberg shows how charming he can be. Under the guise of making polite conversation he finds out who Meg's guest is, but when she tries to tell him about the concert Stanley gave, she is unable to remember much about it. The unreliability of her memory here makes us wonder how accurate her recollections are elsewhere in the play.

The plot develops when Meg announces that it is Stanley's birthday. Goldberg's decision that he must have a party delights Meg, and is another example of his ability to deflect suspicion by appearing to be generous and scrupulous in his regard for tradition. Meg's remark that a party will cheer Stanley up is particularly ironic, especially as two of the guests are people he seeks to avoid and a third, Lulu, is someone who thinks he is a complete failure. All the ingredients are there for an awkward, grotesque celebration.

Take a holiday . . . Look at me Pinter establishes Goldberg's dominance partly by having him speak in clipped sentences beginning with a command.

Brighton, Canvey Island, Rottingdean Canvey Island is in the Thames estuary. Brighton and Rottingdean are on the Sussex coast.

Shabbuss The Jewish word for Sabbath.

Basingstoke By mentioning this town in Hampshire, Goldberg leads us to believe that his Uncle Barney was the essence of respectability.

You know one thing . . . very busy man As with Stanley's speech about the concert, we have no way of verifying what Goldberg says, except by what he does in the play. Although he speaks here of a son, he does not behave like a family man, and his insistence upon being a gentleman does not square with his treatment of Lulu.

We were after a nice place, you understand. So we came to you Goldberg unerringly realizes how a compliment like this will flatter Meg.

He hasn't mentioned it We are left uncertain at this stage about whether it actually is Stanley's birthday or whether Meg merely thinks it is. It is another means by which the atmosphere of ambiguous uncertainty and menace is generated.

Pages 33–36

On Meg's return downstairs from having shown her guests to their room, she and Stanley have what passes for a conversation but is in fact non-communication. Flushed with success at having guests, Meg is oblivious of Stanley's questions about the men which become more and more insistent. Meg's failure to remember their names not only helps confirm the weakness of her memory but also underlines how inefficient a businesswoman she is. When she finally remembers Goldberg's name, Stanley's response is significant; he sits in silence at the table, as though unaware of Meg's continuing prattle. Why the name should have such an effect upon him is a mystery. It not only helps create an atmosphere of dramatic menace, but also increases our curiosity. We would like an authoritative explanation because we feel more comfortable with what we know but, as so often in real life, we are not given one.

When Meg tells him that it is his birthday, Stanley denies it, but his usual assertiveness has deserted him. Dumbfounded by the information Meg has given him, he abjectly obeys her request to open his present. It is a toy drum, bought for him by Meg because he no longer has a piano. It is an example of her kindness, her stupidity, and her treatment of Stanley as a child. As the act moves towards its conclusion, Stanley marches round the table beating the drum more and more savagely. Here he shows his physical aggression (up to now he has been violent only in his language) – and prepares us for his attack upon Lulu at the end of Act Two. It is an excellent example of the careful construction of the play, for while Pinter explains very little, he prepares us meticulously for what actually happens on stage.

Revision questions and assignments on Act One

1 By carefully referring to specific incidents in the act, show how Pinter establishes an atmosphere of menace.

2 Discuss briefly Meg's attitude toward Stanley and his toward her.

3 Write a character study of Goldberg paying particular attention to the way in which he behaves toward (a) McCann; (b) Stanley; (c) Meg.

4 Show how Pinter uses the way people speak as a guide to their character.

Act Two

Pages 37–42

This section deals with Stanley's attempts to find out more about McCann. Although it has its comic moments, it seethes with suppressed fear and violence. McCann's pastime of tearing sheets of newspaper into equal strips gives a clear insight into his character: unimaginative, methodical and destructive. Pinter quickly establishes the undercurrent of menace. At first it is hinted at through a series of minor details which, on the surface, suggest good manners: McCann's rising to intercept Stanley on the pretext of wishing to introduce himself; the way in which he grips Stanley's hand for too long in the handshake; the way in which he contradicts Stanley's remark that it is unfortunate that Stanley will not be present at the party. Much of the dialogue consists in the kind of empty remarks strangers make to each other to pass the time, but Pinter brilliantly invests such banalities with undefined but very real menace. Ill at ease, Stanley decides to take the battle to McCann by joining him in whistling the tune 'The Mountains of Mourne'. The result is a remarkable dramatic moment – simultaneously comic and highly unnerving – as two grown men face each other whistling together, and then whistle alternately as the other speaks. On one level it is like an amusing comedy sketch showing how silly two adults can be; on another it is like a primitive test of strength.

McCann's suppressed aggression becomes more obvious when he warns Stanley off touching the newspaper he has been tearing. Once more, Stanley interrogates McCann who gives little away. He admits that he has never met Stanley before, but the effect he has upon Stanley is evident in the latter's three comparatively long speeches. These are worth close attention because in an obscure but very real way Stanley tries to placate McCann by showing him that he is not the kind of person to cause any trouble. He behaves like a pupil before a headteacher. Pinter does not tell us why McCann should have this effect upon Stanley – it is another deliberate ambiguity in the play; the more we search for a precise reason the more it evades us. Perhaps

Pinter is suggesting that we all have a guilty secret in our past, a secret that makes us frightened of strangers or figures who combine authority and threat. His attempt to explain himself having failed, Stanley resorts to questioning McCann whose warnings about Stanley getting too close to his paper become increasingly menacing. The menace, which has so far been present in the language only, bursts briefly into the action when McCann savagely hits Stanley's arm. Stanley's further attempts to placate McCann fail, but they emphasize his conviction that McCann and Goldberg have come to get him for something he has done in the past.

But it is an honour . . . Ah no. This short interchange is an example of the way menace is generated through McCann's quiet insistence.

Boots Library As well as being chemists, Boots at one time ran a library service. By mentioning such ordinary things as the library, the teashop and the High Street, Stanley is trying to show McCann how respectable and normal he is.

You know what? . . . Do you know what I mean? Stanley's broken phrases show the strain he is under. He feels compelled to offer some kind of explanation, but cannot find the words.

Pages 42–44

With the entry of Petey and Goldberg, the tone of the act changes markedly. Goldberg's easy fluency contrasts with the grim brevity of McCann, as does the topic of his conversation. Once more, he has been reminiscing, this time to Petey. He conjures up a world of innocent courtship, happiness, kindness to one's fellows, love of one's mother, and the simple pleasures of childhood. Petey announces that he will miss the party as he has a chess match, and leaves to Goldberg's fulsome wish that he beat his opponent quickly and return.

I was telling Mr Boles . . . the dog stadium. An important speech which shows how Goldberg relies on clichés to present a cosy picture of the past. However, Pinter implies that there is something fake about Goldberg's happy reminiscences: adults have never tipped their hats – a sign of respect – to toddlers; and the idea of giving a helping hand to a couple of dogs is comic rather than realistic, as is what he intends to be the romantic picture of the sun setting on the dog stadium. By having Goldberg use details in such an inappropriate way, Pinter achieves two things: first, he reminds us that Goldberg is a comic character as well as an enigmatic, though frightening, one; second, he shows that Goldberg is not what he pretends to be.

Carrikmacross McCann's home in Ireland.

There's no comparison. Goldberg's recollection of *his* past has prompted McCann to think of his home. However, Goldberg's curt dismissal shows a cruel side to him, at odds with the impression he is trying to give.

gefilte fish Chopped fish cooked with egg and served cold; a Jewish recipe.

Mention my name. Goldberg is trying to impress Petey by telling McCann that mere mention of his name will ensure special service.

Pages 44–53

Briefly left alone with Goldberg, Stanley tries to get rid of him. Goldberg easily brushes aside his attempts, first by congratulating him on his birthday and secondly by talking at length about his own health. When McCann returns with bottles for the party, the dialogue takes on a grotesque tone of comic menace unique to Pinter. Stanley's attempts at self-assertion, though they work with Meg, are quite inadequate against McCann and Goldberg. The routine in which McCann asks Stanley to sit down and then reports his progress to Goldberg is reminiscent of slapstick comedy, except that its tone is charged with the possibility of violence. As their intentions toward Stanley become more openly hostile, we note that their language becomes less refined.

Once Stanley is sitting, a remarkable interrogation begins in which a series of quick-fire questions, ranging from the trivial (where does Stanley keep his suits?) to the sinister (why did he leave the organization?), from the absurd to the serious, disorientate Stanley and throw him on the defensive. McCann's question about leaving the organization, together with later accusations that Stanley betrayed McCann's land and Goldberg's breed, appears to offer a specific explanation of why they want Stanley – he has actually betrayed an organization for which they work. However, these accusations are only a few among many others. Pinter does not wish to give a clear, unambiguous reason for their arrival. By never fully clarifying the motives of McCann and Goldberg, Pinter makes the action more universally applicable; not everyone has betrayed an organization, but everyone has done something of which they are ashamed and are fearful of being exposed.

Then, at Goldberg's command, McCann removes Stanley's glasses and moves his chair downstage. Stanley, now half-blind, stumbles after it and clutches it for safety. Once they have him in this abject position, McCann and Goldberg continue their nightmare interrogation. With only a few exceptions, all of the speeches in the rest of this section comprise a single line so that the speed of delivery and the oddity of their content break Stanley down completely. That the inquisition follows no logical pattern makes it all the more effective. For instance, Stanley is at one point accused of murdering his wife only moments later to be told that he never married but left his fiancée pregnant, waiting at the church. The recurring theme is Stanley's inadequacy, treachery, uncleanliness. He becomes so disorientated that he even tries to answer the question about the chicken crossing the road, a fine example of Pinter's investing a joke with menace.

After Stanley's first scream, the interrogation reaches new levels of intensity, concerning itself more consistently with serious accusations and threats. Stanley is accused of betrayal and threatened with death, although the precise nature of his treachery is not made clear. Cornered like an animal and unable to stand any more, he kicks Goldberg and threatens McCann with a chair.

you're beginning to get on my breasts You're beginning to annoy me.
Why are you getting on everybody's wick? Why are you annoying everyone?
Why are you driving that old lady off her conk? 'Conk' is slang for 'nose'. A more usual expression is 'to drive someone off his rocker' (head), but 'conk' – which is the wrong word – underlines Goldberg's foreignness and makes his question both threatening and comic. Notice how Pinter gives Goldberg less refined language here than when he is playing the gentleman in Meg's presence.
the organization As with Meg's 'list' it suggests power and authority, vaguely understood but able to influence people's lives.
Black and Tan A semi-military police force founded in Ireland in 1920 for the suppression of the IRA. McCann's reference to them here might indicate that he is a member of the IRA, although as stated above, Pinter usually avoids being specific in this way.
Enos or Andrews Brands of liver salts. Goldberg's insistence on knowing if they did or didn't fizz is at once comic and threatening.
In – Stanley starts to answer the question, 'Where was your wife?' Note that from here on, Stanley's responses become less frequent, often

monosyllabic and unsure. Quick-fire questioning like this *can* lead to the truth, but it can also be so confusing that victims become dumb or begin to admit to what is not true.

Right? . . . all along the line. Goldberg's 'logic' is not meant to make any sense, but it is intended to impress upon Stanley that whatever he says is right and whatever Stanley says is wrong.

the cloth The clergy.

Albigensenist heresy Albigensenists were religious heretics in medieval France. That someone like McCann should know about this obscure detail is, of course, comic. But it also raises questions about McCann himself. Goldberg claims in Act Three that McCann is an unfrocked priest; this is the kind of thing a Catholic priest might know. McCann's question therefore functions as another piece of Pinter ambiguity.

watered the wicket in Melbourne Tampered with a cricket pitch before a Test match. Cricket features largely in Goldberg's speeches. It is one way in which he attempts to pass himself off as a fully integrated Englishman.

blessed Oliver Plunkett A Catholic martyr accused of plotting against King Charles II; the last Catholic to be executed in England.

Drogheda An Irish uprising against English rule in 1649 was brutally suppressed at Drogheda by Oliver Cromwell. Both this reference and the one above show McCann's strong Irish, and therefore anti-English, sympathy.

Pages 53–63

The entry of Meg, in evening dress and holding the drum, signals another abrupt change of tone. A convivial party atmosphere is quickly established, completely at odds with what has just happened. Goldberg reverts without effort to his other role as sauve master of ceremonies. He compliments Meg and insists that she propose the toast to Stanley. Her speech is banal in the extreme as she is incapable of expressing strong emotions but it is none the less a sincere expression of her deep fondness for Stanley. Lulu arrives in time for the toast.

Goldberg is fulsome in his praise of Meg's speech, and nostalgic about the past and his own simple pleasures, noticeably conventional. He insists that the toast be drunk in darkness with torchlight shining on Stanley's face. In dramatic terms this is another effective piece of ambiguity. While apparently wishing Stanley well, by trapping him in a beam of light Goldberg reminds him that there is no escape.

Lulu, who in Act One found Stanley's reticence disappointing, is quite openly attracted to Goldberg and expresses her admiration of his eloquence. His response, where he describes the success of his lecture at the Ethical Hall, is remarkably similar to Stanley's account in Act One of his piano concert in Lower Edmonton (compare the two). The improbability of both stories hints that Goldberg and Stanley, different in so many ways, both need to create a past for themselves; Stanley because he is an unmotivated failure, Goldberg because, as a Jew and therefore an outsider in a Christian country, he needs to present himself as both successful and fully integrated.

As the party progresses, Stanley, ironically, is forgotten. Lulu is so attracted to Goldberg that she accepts his invitation to sit on his lap, while he tells her about his late wife. His account of his married life presents the same idyllic picture of bliss as his earlier account of his youth. While the flirtations of Lulu and Goldberg become more openly suggestive, McCann and Meg reminisce about their respective pasts, as much to themselves as to each other. Like Goldberg, each of them looks to the past as a time of comfort, security and happiness. The important point is not whether or not their recollections are accurate, but the need they have of happy memories to comfort them now. McCann, who is getting progressively more sentimental with drink, sings an Irish ballad. Meg's announcement that she wants to play a game brings Stanley, who has been sulking, back into the picture.

Doesn't it make a beautiful noise? Meg's remark that a toy drum makes a beautiful noise shows her stupidity and Pinter's cutting humour.

one bottle of Irish Irish whiskey. As an Irish patriot, McCann will not drink Scotch.

a little Austin A type of small, ordinary car – another telling detail in the solid, respectable image of himself that Goldberg presents.

tea in Fullers, a library book from Boots Fullers was a rather smart chain of teashops famous for their cakes. In order to show how simple and unadventurous his life was, Goldberg chooses exactly those details that Stanley had mentioned earlier to McCann. Pinter makes us wonder if it is mere accident, or whether Goldberg has some kind of intuitive knowledge. By such a device he generates more mystery and ambiguity around the figure of Goldberg.

Mazoltov Good luck.

Simchahs Happy events. Goldberg's use of these two Hebrew words remind us of his Jewishness.

The Necessary and the Possible In the midst of the party, Goldberg is being deliberately obscure in order to cause confusion.

Ever been to Carrikmacross? ... King's Cross A fine example of Pinter's command of the anti-climax as the means of a joke – the confusion of two places that rhyme. King's Cross is a railway station in London.

I'd say hullo ... She called me Simey Notice the similarity between this story involving Goldberg's wife and the one earlier involving his mother. Even though Jews lay great stress on the importance of family life and the continuity of tradition, Goldberg's stories of idyllic family happiness are told in such similar terms that we suspect he is more concerned with presenting a favourable image of himself than with telling the truth.

Fenian A group of Irish patriots formed in the nineteenth century to overthrow English domination of Ireland. This could provide further proof of McCann's Irish republican sympathies. Equally, given that he is drunk, it could be merely a snatch of song that he sings.

Pages 63–66

Although a game of Blind Man's Buff seems innocent enough, there are indications from the start that matters are getting out of hand. Parties are, by their very nature, occasions for people to act informally, but Pinter uses such an occasion to strip human beings of the civilized restraint normally expected of them and expose the violent and manipulative behaviour of which they are capable. Two stage directions, for instance – those showing Goldberg fondling Lulu – indicate how indiscreet he is being in his seduction of her. Then McCann takes Stanley's glasses, recalling the interrogation Stanley underwent earlier in the act (which was, in one sense, another game of blind man's buff). Stanley is here the victim again. The atmosphere of menace increases quickly when, with Stanley literally blind for the moment, McCann breaks his glasses, Lulu and Goldberg close together, and McCann makes Stanley trip over by putting the drum in his way. Menace gives way to open violence when Stanley, whose potential for violence was indicated in the way he beat the drum at the end of Act One, tries to throttle Meg until he is thrown off by Goldberg and McCann.

Tension mounts when a sudden blackout throws the entire

room into darkness. The game of Blind Man's Buff has now taken a sinister turn, for all of the characters are unable to see. We learn later that the blackout has been caused only by the electricity meter running out of money, but at the time it happens it offers an example of how Pinter can generate menace from ordinary domestic events. In the confusion, Stanley finds Lulu and places her on the table. When McCann recovers the torch and shines it on the table, Lulu is lying spread-eagled with Stanley bending over her. The entire incident is ambiguous. Does she think it is Goldberg who put her on the table in order to seduce her? Does Stanley intend to rape her? Pinter does not tell us, and in this way creates a tension between our very human desire to know and the inadequacy of the evidence with which we are presented.

Stanley, caught in the torchlight in a compromising position, backs away to the wall, giggling as he does so (note that giggles often indicate nervousness). McCann and Goldberg converge threateningly on him.

He begins to strangle her As Stanley is blindfolded, he cannot see whom he is strangling. The point is that the eternal victim is willing, in turn, to victimize others.

He backs, giggling, the torch on his face Pinter's use of this scene in conjunction with the earlier one involving the torch shows what a careful craftsman he is as well as having an unerring eye for dramatic effect. The mood of the earlier scene is one of suppressed menace; here that menace is given more overt expression. By using these two scenes as points of comparison, Pinter shows us how the tension rises until Goldberg and McCann have Stanley against a wall like a trapped animal.

Revision questions and assignments on Act Two

1 As well as being threatening, this act is also comic. Discuss how Pinter manages to blend these two features.

2 What do we learn of Stanley in this act?

3 Write a brief essay showing how the past features in this act.

4 How effective do you think this act would be on stage?

5 Show that although all the elements one associates with a party are present they go disturbingly wrong.

Act Three

Pages 67–79

After the climax of the party, Pinter allows the tension to drop. The next morning there is the same kind of banal conversation between Petey and Meg that there was at the start of the play. Meg can remember little about the party and complains about a headache. When she mentions calling Stanley, Petey is quick to discourage her, alerting us to the possibility that he knows something Meg does not. His mention of there being a large car outside awakens fear in Meg of Stanley's story in Act One of men with a wheelbarrow. She is reassured when Petey tells her that it is Goldberg's car. This reassurance is, of course, ironic as she sees no threat in Goldberg. Goldberg enters from upstairs just before Meg goes shopping. Although he is full of compliments for her, we notice that he ignores her obvious hint about a ride to the shops and drinks his tea instead. Clearly he feels he needs to be present in the house with McCann and Stanley. Left alone together, Goldberg and Petey discuss Stanley, who, according to Goldberg, has had a nervous breakdown and is being cared for upstairs by McCann. When Petey questions him further about the speed of the breakdown, Goldberg is less self-assured than usual. This uncertainty is a new, and revealing, aspect of his character.

When McCann enters with suitcases, he is sullen toward Goldberg. Once again, Pinter arouses our curiosity by this change in their relationship but does not give us a clear reason; it seems to be connected with what has been happening to Stanley. McCann's refusal to go back upstairs, together with his remark that Stanley is now quiet, strikes an ominous note. Yet although we inevitably think that McCann has been mistreating Stanley upstairs, there is no clear, irrefutable evidence. It is possible that Stanley's behaviour is so disturbed that McCann feels unwilling to be in the same room with him All we can do is speculate, always aware that like Goldberg and McCann when the lights went out, we are groping in the dark. For example, McCann's reluctance to go back upstairs could be because he feels angry that Goldberg spent the night with Lulu and left him to do the unpleasant work of breaking down Stanley; or it could be that he feels disgust at what he has done. Either is possible.

Petey's character continues to develop as he shows concern for

Stanley's welfare. Normally compliant and easy-going, Petey demonstrates a quiet strength here, as he does a little later when, despite Goldberg's insistence that he return to his job, he calmly states that he is going to do some gardening. He clearly suspects the circumstances under which Stanley is leaving the house.

When they are left alone, there is an extraordinary sequence of events between Goldberg and McCann. Goldberg is clearly on edge; he brusquely tells McCann to stop tearing newspaper into strips. When McCann asks for instructions, Goldberg seems too exhausted to give any. Pinter here develops the side of Goldberg's character he introduced earlier in the section. Normally self-assured and dominant, he is now indecisive. McCann's urgings that they finish the job show Pinter using ambiguity for dramatic effect. Exactly what he means is not made clear, although it is quite possible that he means they should kill Stanley.

Getting no response from Goldberg, McCann makes the error of calling him Simey, a name used, according to Goldberg, only by his wife and mother. Goldberg's response is terrifying. From being lethargic, he becomes murderous, gripping McCann by the throat and demanding that he never be called that again. Why the name should provide such a strong response is something we have to deduce for ourselves; perhaps it is because the name is more obviously Jewish than either Nat or Benny (other names by which he is known), and his Jewishness is something which Goldberg tries (unsuccessfully) to conceal.

This incident is followed by a bizarre passage in which Goldberg beckons McCann to him, opens his mouth, and asks McCann to look inside. He wants to convince McCann of his excellent health! His health is clearly important to him, and appears to be bound up both with his idea of success and with his self-identity. The first of two long speeches he makes begins in the usual way, showing nostalgia for the past and for traditional values (note the cricketing metaphors). However, as he proceeds in his self-justifying speech, he breaks down, unable to find the words to carry on. It is important to note which sentence it is that he cannot finish; presumably he cannot say what he believes about the world because he has no beliefs. For all his glibness, there is no centre to Goldberg, only an unbroken series of gestures and a succession of clichés.

He recovers, however, to tell McCann about his dying father.

Once more the emphasis is upon the old-fashioned virtues of respect, loyalty, clean living and duty. By the time he closes his speech, he has talked himself back into self-assurance, but his empty platitudes to McCann do little to convince us that there is anything more than a gaping hollow at the centre of Goldberg. Then, in a strange ritual, he asks McCann to blow twice into his mouth. He does not explain why he should find this invigorating, but it is possible that Goldberg literally needs a breath of McCann's simple brute force to steady him; or because, as a Christian, McCann can in some way legitimize Goldberg's attempts to integrate himself; or because, as an Irish Catholic and a Jew, they belong to racial minorities and this gesture represents a kind of communion to Goldberg. The incident is at once highly ritualistic in its action and ambiguous in its precise meaning. What it does show, though, is the inextricable nature of the relationship between the two; Goldberg needs McCann just as much as McCann needs him.

That big car Despite Goldberg's statement that a small Austin was all he needed, he drives a big car.

Put a shilling in the slot Meg and Petey pay for their electricity as they use it.

Follow my mental? Understand what I'm saying?

Play up, play up, and play the game From a heroic poem by the Victorian poet Sir Henry Newbolt. It praises the way in which public school cricket instils courage, honour and teamsmanship and prepares young men for glory in battle. Its patriotic sentiments are a far cry from Goldberg, as are his other cricketing metaphors in this speech.

schnorrers Tricksters.

Seamus Earlier in the act Petey called McCann Dermot. Goldberg's calling him Seamus here means we're not even sure of his first name.

Pages 79–81

When Lulu enters, we learn that she and Goldberg have spent the night together, and she is filled with self-disgust. Goldberg is unperturbed by her recriminations. We see Goldberg once again as the exploiter of others, his cavalier treatment of Lulu sitting uneasily with the pious sentiments he expresses elsehwere. When McCann returns from upstairs, he shows another side of his character: strong sexual morality. He is contemptuous of Lulu, and urges her to confess her sins to him. Goldberg's remark that McCann is a recently defrocked Catholic priest is probably a joke intended to mock Lulu; however, Pinter leaves us unsure even of this.

Pages 81–87

Just after Lulu exits, McCann brings in Stanley, now clean shaven and well dressed. He is carrying his broken glasses, the symbol of his subjugation. Goldberg and McCann proceed to soothe him in a long sequence of one-line promises, many of them absurd. It presents a variation upon the quick-fire interrogation they used in Act Two, although its intention is less to frighten Stanley than to convince him of his dependence on them. Utterly defeated, Stanley remains unresponsive throughout, and when asked to speak can make only a few childish, incomprehensible utterances. He has been stripped by McCann and Goldberg of any ability to function as an autonomous human being.

As they are about to take Stanley away, Petey enters and, sensing that something is most decidedly wrong, insists that Stanley remain behind. Petey's concern for Stanley contrasts here with the mocking callousness of Goldberg and McCann. However, his determination wavers when Goldberg invites him to join them in their visit to the doctor. On the surface, there is nothing disturbing about the invitation, but it is part of Pinter's genius to endow such a seemingly normal offer with menace. It represents a test of Petey's courage to stand by what he feels is right. Frightened, Petey does nothing. Unable to stand up for Stanley, he ironically asks Stanley to do it himself. As with so much of the play, we feel that the incident is at once of particular significance (what it tells us about Petey), and of general importance, too (what it tells us about how fear can overcome decency in anyone).

Having failed the test, Petey appears to be unaffected by it. Instead, he resumes his normal life, picking up the paper and reading it. When Meg returns from her shopping, he pretends everything is normal and that Stanley is still asleep upstairs. However, the pauses in his speech indicate that he knows the truth and is keeping it from her because he cannot bear to see her hurt. Meg's prattle about what a lovely party it was and how she was the belle of the ball is, of course, totally at odds with what actually happened. She cannot even remember that Petey was not there. The play closes on the same level of banality on which it opened. We do not know how Meg will respond when she finds Stanley gone, or whether she will even remember clearly that he was ever there. The victim of a treacherous memory, Meg is unable truly to evaluate her past and therefore cannot understand the present.

fast days ... kneeling days Holy days when one either eats nothing (fasts) or kneels in prayer.
constitutionals Healthy walks.
mensch (Hebrew) Fine figure of a man.
The prayer wheel A revolving box containing prayers used by Buddhists. After a list of details concerning Stanley's physical health, McCann is hinting that they will look after his spiritual welfare too.

Revision questions and assignments on Act Three

1 Consider the role of Petey in this act.

2 Show how Pinter creates ambiguity in our minds about what has happened to Stanley.

3 Confining your answer only to this act, write a character study of Goldberg, showing in particular how he relates to McCann and Petey.

4 Why do you think Pinter ends the play as he does? Do you find it a successful ending?

Pinter's art in *The Birthday Party*
Characters

The characters in *The Birthday Party* fall into two broad groups. Those of the first, Meg, Lulu and Petey, are 'knowable' in that there are certain identifiable and verifiable facts about them. For example, we never question that Meg runs a boarding house, that Petey works as a deckchair attendant, and that Lulu is a neighbour. We come to know a great deal about them, the kind of people they are, their daily routine, their hopes and fears. The other group, comprising Stanley, McCann and Goldberg, is 'unknowable'. In dramatizing their characters, Pinter generates a creative tension between our desire for answers and his refusal to tell us. For instance, why Goldberg and McCann have come to get Stanley remains a mystery. We never find out who they are, just as we never know what has made Stanley the failure he is.

Stanley

a bit of a washout

A shabby figure in his late thirties, Stanley is one of life's failures: he is unable to impose any order upon his life or to act with any purpose. There is a noticeable element of emotional immaturity in him, especially in the way he behaves with Meg. It is true that she treats him as though he were a child, but he allows himself to be treated in this way. Although he professes to despise it, he needs this relationship of smothering love and attention, just as much as Meg does. In Meg, and in Petey, too, Stanley has found substitute parents who will tolerate all his bad behaviour because they love him.

Safe in Meg's house, with nothing expected of him, Stanley feels secure in his rejection of life and relationships. When Lulu expresses interest in him in Act One, he shows his immaturity by his ridiculous, childish boasting to her and then by backing away from any commitment; he will not even go for a walk with her. Instead of actually embracing life, he shuns it, dreaming instead of a future that will never happen. His lofty claims to Meg of touring the capitals of Europe playing the piano are obviously nothing more than fantasies. He lacks even the energy to sustain his boasts of the future; all his grand dreams give way to recollections of a mundane – and almost certainly fictitious – success in the past, a concert at Lower Edmonton.

However, Stanley's character is by no means easy to fathom. It is when he talks of his past (as he also does to McCann in Act Two), and has his past talked about, that he becomes most ambiguous and mysterious. Pinter denies us the means of verifying the events of Stanley's past and this makes him just as impenetrable as Goldberg and McCann. There is, for instance, no clear evidence that he can play the piano at all; we never see him play anything other than a toy drum. Meg says that she used to enjoy watching him play the piano, but her ability to differentiate between fact and fiction is unreliable.

As the play progresses, we become less, not more, certain about who Stanley actually is, and why he behaves as he does. For example, there are several possible explanations for his anxiety when he hears two strangers are coming. It could be because he fears that he will no longer be the centre of Meg's attentions; it could equally be because he actually has done something in the past for which he is being hunted – his behaviour in Act One when Meg tells him Goldberg's name makes this a possibility; it could be that he is so anti-social and conservative that any threat to the status quo makes him nervous; it could be that he thinks the two gentlemen are representatives of respectable society whose purpose is to make him respectable too; or it could be that he has a dark and obscure fear of being exposed for the kind of person he is – slothful, filled with hatred and a primitive sexuality that cannot express itself in ordinary, conventional activities like taking Lulu for a walk. It is a remarkable achievement of Pinter to make this evident failure so unknowable beyond what we see and hear of him in the play.

Whatever else Goldberg and McCann do, they expose fully the elements of suppressed violence and sexuality in Stanley's character and reduce him to a human wreck. The potential for violence is there from the outset in the way he speaks to Meg, and then, more obviously, in his manner of beating the drum at the end of Act One. But it is at the party, after the interrogation in which Goldberg and McCann degrade him, that the full extent of his violence becomes apparent when he attempts to throttle Meg and rape Lulu.

When he appears in Act Three, Stanley is clean, presentable and conventionally dressed. Having been destroyed as an individual and rendered incapable of articulate response, he is offered by Goldberg and McCann the things he needs to be a success in society. Earlier in the play, Stanley was at least an individual; at the end he is little better than an automaton. Whether Goldberg actually intends to take him to a doctor or to have McCann kill him (as is implied in Act One) does not matter; Stanley has ceased to function as a human being.

Meg

'Wasn't it a lovely party last night?'

A woman in her sixties, Meg is motherly, generous, sentimental, unobservant and stupid. She prides herself on being a good wife and landlady, although all the evidence suggests otherwise. Her remarks to Petey early in Act One are banal and obvious, said for something to say rather than to communicate any ideas or information. With Stanley, however, she is different. The fact that she treats him like a small boy shows that her need to express the maternal side of her nature is stronger than the evidence of her eyes – Stanley is a grown man. Conflicting with this is the way in which she flirts with Stanley and therefore obviously sees him as a man.

Being gullible, she is easily taken in by Goldberg's smooth-talking. His suggestion that they have a party brings out a child-like delight in her. After she has shown Goldberg and McCann to their room, she reveals two of her central characteristics in her conversation with Stanley: first, her hopelessness as a landlady – she has no idea how long they are staying and struggles to remember Goldberg's name; secondly, her stupid but genuine kindness when she gives Stanley his birthday present early to cheer him up. That the present is both inappropriate and possibly untimely (Stanley denies it is his birthday) is typical of Meg's blundering generosity.

The evening dress she wears for the party shows how special such an occasion is for her, but also demonstrates her high regard for Stanley. Manoeuvred by Goldberg into making a speech, Pinter makes her usual struggle with language into a very moving occasion. Unable to fashion words in the glib but hollow way that Goldberg does, Meg's simple clichés are moving because they are sincere. After her heroic feat, she drinks too much and falls into maudlin reminiscence with McCann. Her memories about being a little girl might be no more than fantasy – typically Pinter does not allow us to verify the truth or otherwise of Meg's past – but they do show us her deep yearning to be cherished. It is on occasions like this that Meg becomes far more than just an empty-headed woman. We glimpse a human being with a deep-rooted need for love and company which will never be satisfied.

The morning after the party, Meg finds it difficult to relate cause and effect. She does not know why she has a headache, and thinks she slept heavily because she was tired, whereas the truth is obvious: she had too much to drink. Her failure to remember how the drum was broken shows once again the unreliability of her memory. She cannot cope with unpalatable truths.

Generally very unobservant, Meg does notice the big car parked outside. Her reason for doing so is at once comic and very touching. The comedy resides in her asking Petey if there is a wheelbarrow inside, a question which takes even him by surprise. It is touching because we realize that Stanley's attempt to frighten her in Act One has actually worked. Instead of dismissing the story as preposterous, as any normal person would do, Meg has believed it, and through this we get a glimpse of someone who is not only gullible but for whom the world can suddenly become very threatening; just as it does for Stanley. By the time she returns from shopping, Stanley has gone. With Petey bearing the secret he knows will upset her deeply, Meg prattles on about what a wonderful party it was, showing how little she understood what actually happened.

Petey

'We all remember our childhood'

Petey is a kind, decent man who shows loyalty, if not love, to Meg, but who at the end of the play is found wanting when his courage is tested by Goldberg. At the outset of the play, Pinter shows the tedium of Petey and Meg's marriage. They have nothing to say to each other. Petey behaves kindly to Meg, however. He is patient when dealing with her inane questions, and, if he objects to the unappetizing breakfast she has made him, he does not complain. In this he presents a notable contrast to Stanley, who treats Meg in a far more aggressive and impolite manner.

After Petey leaves for work in Act One, he is not seen again until Act Two, and then only briefly. Goldberg's remark that he has been talking about his mother to Petey while they walked about the garden suggests another important facet of Petey's character; he is a listener rather than a talker, and a reflective person rather than someone who acts (note that he misses the party because he has a chess game). Petey, then, misses the central sequence of the play. It is possible that Pinter is implying that Petey is fated to live on the sidelines of life; by some quirk of circumstance or destiny, he is never actually present on occasions in which lives are challenged and changed.

Though docile and self-effacing, Petey is practical (he realizes that the blackout at Stanley's party is nothing more than a shortage of money in the meter) and not unobservant. In Act Three he is uneasy about Stanley, quickly discouraging Meg from waking him, and showing eagerness to get her out of the house shopping because he does not want her to be upset by Stanley's breakdown. He even manages to ruffle Goldberg with his quiet but insistent remarks about Stanley. This determined side to his character becomes more apparent when he refuses to respond to Goldberg's encouragement to return to work and says he is going into the garden. We get the impression that Petey is uneasy about what Goldberg and McCann intend to do to Stanley and wishes to observe them closely. When Stanley is finally brought downstairs, Petey's simple kindness contrasts with the callous plans of Goldberg and McCann. As Petey's suspicions grow, he acts decisively for the only time in the play, demanding that Stanley be left alone. The courage he displays here is real, but momentary. When Goldberg challenges him, by inviting him to accompany Stanley to the doctor, Petey crumbles, pathetically urging Stanley to stand up to them in a way that he himself is unable to do. When Meg returns, Petey relapses into his docile, emollient self, hiding from her the fact that Stanley has gone, and speaking sympathetically though uninterestedly to her.

Lulu

a big, bouncy girl

Like Petey, Lulu is one of the minor characters. As her name suggests, she is flirtatious and empty-headed. On her first appearance, she shows a willingness to engage Stanley in conversation and is curious about how he spends his time. Her offer to go for a walk with him shows her willingness to take the initiative in such matters but Stanley is a disappointment and declines. Her dismissive remark to Stanley as she leaves is as much a sexual insult as anything else.

Goldberg, however, wins an entirely different response from her. At the party, his glib, easy manner impresses her, and sensing that Goldberg is far more worldly than Stanley she quickly accepts his invitation to sit on his lap. As the party proceeds, her flirting becomes more obviously laden with sexual innuendo and intent: the implication behind her comments that she has always liked older men and that Goldberg resembles the first man she ever loved are not lost on someone as opportunistic as he is.

However, although Lulu might present herself as worldly, she is none the less a victim of man's rapacity and cruelty. Under cover of darkness at the party, Stanley advances on her and tries to assault her. Later, in Act Three, after she has spent the night with Goldberg she is disgusted with herself, but he treats her with dismissive mockery. In the same scene, McCann savagely demands that she confess her sins to him.

In Lulu, then, Pinter creates a character who appears to be self-assured and worldly, but who suffers at the hands of three of the four men in the play. To some extent she asks for trouble because of the blatant way she flaunts herself. However, there is nothing vicious about Lulu. All she wants is some fun; what she gets from Stanley, Goldberg and McCann is far more threatening.

Goldberg

'I believe in a good laugh, a day's fishing, a bit of gardening'

In a play in which so many characters find language and communication a problem, Goldberg has a way with words which immediately marks him out as a force to be contended with. Yet

Pinter uses Goldberg's fluency to conceal rather than reveal. The more Goldberg talks about the cosiness of the past, and his respect for family and traditional values, the more inexplicable he becomes, for his behaviour towards both Stanley and Lulu runs counter to the picture of himself he tries to create.

When he and McCann enter in Act One, he is quickly established as the dominant partner – it is, for instance, McCann who carries both suitcases. His self-satisfied, glib remarks about idyllic days spent with his Uncle Barney, and the emphasis he puts upon being a gentleman, suggest first of all that, as a Jew, Goldberg is anxious to show himself as being fully integrated into the English way of life.

He finds it easy to charm Meg. Just after he meets her he interrogates her gently but efficiently about who is staying at her house; this contrasts with his more aggressive questioning of Stanley and shows how versatile – and therefore dangerous – he can be. When Meg tells him it is Stanley's birthday, he instantly takes the initiative, proposing a party and complimenting Meg extravagantly, but ridiculously, on the way she will look in her best dress. Clearly, his intention here is to give an impression of bonhomie so that any suspicions Meg might have are allayed.

He does the same sort of thing with Petey, too, early in Act Two, by talking nostalgically about his young manhood. Yet for all his glibness, Goldberg's language betrays him. He speaks of tipping his hat to toddlers, giving a helping hand to stray dogs, behaviour which would be appropriate for a gentleman to a lady, but is ridiculous here.

When Goldberg and McCann subject Stanley to their interrogation in Act Two, the brutal, relentless side of his character is exposed. The questions he fires at Stanley are sometimes absurd, sometimes serious, but always insistent and threatening. It is perhaps here that Goldberg is most clearly seen as a comic and a threatening figure at one and the same time.

During the party itself, his false sentiments contrast with Meg's sincerity. He impresses Lulu as easily as he earlier impressed Meg, but his attitude toward her presents us with another ambiguity. For all the respectful way he speaks of women elsewhere, he is quick to exploit Lulu despite the fact that she is some thirty years his junior. At first, he shows himself an adept though flashy ladies' man, making flirtatious remarks which carry strong sexual overtones. Then he wins her sympathy by the sentimental way he speaks of his dead wife (while actually seducing Lulu). Later, in Act Three, Lulu's horror at the way he behaved when they spent the night together shows what a ruthless, exploitative character Goldberg is.

It is in Act Three that Goldberg's smooth façade momentarily breaks down, and we have a glimpse of the terrifying void that lies at the centre of his character. The strain he has been under has a detrimental effect even upon him. In a speech to McCann in which, typically, he boasts of his success in life, the clichés come tumbling out, as though by mouthing these comforting platitudes he will reassure himself of his own worth. On this occasion they fail, and the most fluent character in the play stumbles into helpless repetition, lost for words and therefore unable to shape his identity.

By the end of the play, we know that Goldberg is violent, threatening, cruel, resourceful, hollow, charming and devious. Yet we still know little about him. How much credence we give to his recollections is debatable; how successful in life he really is we never know.

In Scott Fitzgerald's *The Great Gatsby*, the narrator, Nick Carraway, wonders if 'personality is an unbroken series of successful gestures'. Gestures feature largely in Goldberg. Not all of his gestures are successful, of course – he breaks down in front of McCann for instance, and he is only successful in fooling gullible people like Meg (even Petey becomes suspicious of him by the end). Fitzgerald's quotation implies that personality exists on the surface only, in mannerisms, tones of voice, public behaviour; there is no depth, no essence, nothing to know about the inner life of a person. In this, Goldberg is a triumphant realization of Pinter's ability to suggest a great deal while confirming very little. The more gestures Goldberg makes, the less sure we are of how much credence to give them.

McCann

a capable man

Thirty-year-old McCann is the strong-man in the partnership. Nervous about the job to begin with, he is less articulate than Goldberg and lacks his vulgar charm. His pastime of tearing strips from a newspaper reveals that he is destructive, unimaginative, yet very methodical – the strips he tears are of equal size. However, McCann is not merely a mindless, musclebound thug. For example, his insistence that his invitation to the party is an honour is at once polite and menacing.

His warning to Stanley to stay away from the paper he has torn is more obviously threatening, revealing a primitive, possessive streak in him. However, he is able to control this and to subject Stanley to increasing terror as the scene develops. His terse answers give little away and therefore offer Stanley no comfort. The more hysterical Stanley becomes the more effective McCann's unemotional method of dealing with him becomes. However, when Stanley grips his arm, McCann savagely beats him off, reminding us that the threat he presents is there in his physique as well as in his laconic manner. Taken individually, McCann's comments add up to very little; put together in a sequence of this sort they generate an overwhelming sense of menace. Guided by Goldberg's condescending attitude to McCann at the start, we might have felt condescending toward him too. However, by the start of Act Two we realize that his brute physique together with his ability to generate fear in others make him a formidable opponent.

This is confirmed in the skill with which he complements Goldberg in vilifying Stanley during the interrogation. Never lost for the right word, he usually initiates insults of his own, but sometimes echoes Goldberg's to telling effect. We come to realize that McCann's brevity of speech is not, as with Meg, because his mind is vague but because he instinctively understands the menacing effect of short, clipped utterances. During the questioning of Stanley his references to the Albigensenists and the blessed Oliver Plunkett draw our attention to his Catholicism, while his song about the bold Fenian men at the party hints at Republican sympathies. However, to deduce from this that he is, say, a member of the IRA is to define him in a way that Pinter does not wish. McCann is such a disturbing figure largely because we do not know what his motives are.

What McCann does to Stanley in his bedroom, if he actually does anything, also remains a mystery. However, we get some idea of the dreadful, though unspecified, condition of Stanley from McCann's reluctance to go back upstairs.

As with Goldberg, the greater our desire to know who McCann is and what brings him to Meg's house, the more likely we are to be frustrated. All we finally know about him is that he exudes menace, making even the simple act of tearing paper into strips an exhibition of controlled aggression.

Themes

Themes in a work of literature must not be confused with plot. Whereas the plot is the means of telling the story and is concerned with what happens, the themes are the ideas with which the writer is concerned. The themes of *The Birthday Party* – such as the outsider; violence and power; women, men and sexuality; memories, truth and illusions – feature in other Pinter plays. In presenting these themes, Pinter makes no attempt to tell his audience what to think or which of the themes is most important. In other words, he refuses to be dogmatic about the meaning of his plays. One of his great gifts as a playwright is to suggest to us that what is happening on stage reveals something of significance about life in general, and so it is always tempting to see the characters and action as symbolic of larger, more complex issues.

The Outsider

A seminal Pinter theme is the threat posed to the security of a room and the relationships within it by an outsider who proves to be menacing. In *The Birthday Party* there are two outsiders, McCann and Goldberg. By a brilliantly sustained piece of dramatic ambiguity, Pinter never makes clear who they are or why they have come for Stanley. But the effect they have upon Stanley alters him fundamentally as a human being.

Pinter begins his presentation of this theme by showing how Stanley, in Meg's boarding-house, has carved himself a niche which is, for him, perfect because of its very imperfections. He can be rude to Meg (who, admittedly, is very irritating) without ever being called to account; he can criticize her breakfasts and threaten to leave without ever having his bluff called; he can lie in bed late knowing that she will bring him tea, and so on. In other words, she gives him plenty to complain about while at the same time offering love, attention and even admiration. Like a favoured son, he can get away with virtually anything.

Having established this, Pinter shows the devastating effect the arrival of the two visitors has upon him. By not specifying exactly the reason why they have come, Pinter increases the imaginative and suggestive power of this theme. For instance, at the obvious level, they could be two gangsters who have come to punish Stanley for betraying what they call the organization. At another level, they could be representatives of the state, which expects conformity and sound social behaviour, to bring to heel a member of that society who is individualistic and unsociable. At another, more symbolic level still, they could be embodiments of the kinds of figures who haunt our nightmares, uncannily aware of our weak spots, and able to destroy all our illusions of the past and our hopes for the future. And, most terrifying of all, they can find us wherever we have hidden, and come when we least expect it. Pinter's ability to disturb us comes directly from his use of deliberate vagueness; what is unknown is far more frightening than what is known and classifiable.

Violence and power

Three characters in the play demonstrate this theme: Goldberg, McCann and Stanley. Stanley might seem to be more a victim of violence than a perpetrator, yet Pinter shows how the blanketing love of Meg provokes conflicting responses in him of dependence and resentment; in other words, he depends upon Meg but does not like depending on her. Before the appearance of McCann and Goldberg, his violence goes no further than verbal abuse; once they have stripped him of his illusions, he attacks Meg and attempts to rape Lulu. Unable to relate to a woman of Lulu's age through any of the usual social conventions, such as taking her for a walk, he can demonstrate his manliness only by attempting to assault her. It is a common enough theme in real life, the inadequate man trying to compensate for his inadequacy by treating a woman violently.

However, although Stanley makes a significant contribution to the development of these themes, it is through McCann and Goldberg that they are most elaborately explored. By a mixture of verbal abuse, threats and physical violence, they gain total power over Stanley, relentlessly destroying whatever image of himself he has and replacing it with their own, in which he is a disgusting specimen unworthy of living. Having reduced him in this way, they smarten him up and offer him the trappings of conventional success. Whether they are sincere in this is something Pinter keeps a mystery, and Stanley is too traumatized to care about.

McCann and Goldberg are formidable exponents of the use of violence as a means to power. With Goldberg, power is achieved chiefly through verbal means, taking the form of threats, insults and, before the interrogation when things get really nasty, blithely ignoring what Stanley is saying. A good example of this last technique occurs when Stanley tells him that their room is taken and they will have to leave. Goldberg ignores him and wishes him happy birthday. When Stanley says he must be deaf, Goldberg takes literally what is meant sarcastically and speaks at length on his own fitness. All of Stanley's protests are thus defused.

Goldberg likes power for its own sake. Seeing himself as a man of affairs, he naturally likes to demonstrate his power and influence at every opportunity. For example, he no sooner hears that it is Stanley's birthday than he organizes a party; he exerts his authority over McCann on several occasions; when he sees that Lulu is taken with him, he brutally demonstrates his power over her.

McCann has a more limited view of power than Goldberg. His methodical, unsociable character directs itself toward the removal of Stanley; to do this, power through fear will have to be achieved.

Women, men and sexuality

The two women who appear in the play differ markedly from the perfect specimens – his wife and mother – that exist in Goldberg's imagination. Meg's life with Petey denies her sexual fulfilment and maternal satisfaction; that she is in her sixties does not invalidate either of these desires. Both of these characteristics find expression in her relationship with Stanley to whom her attitude is one of motherly love and clumsily expressed sexual attraction. Pinter here could be dramatizing the idea that any relationship between a man and a woman, even a mother–son relationship is inevitably sexual.

Lulu's sexuality is more obvious partly because she is much younger. Her invitation to Stanley in Act One shows that she is interested in him, even though he does nothing to make himself presentable. At the party, her behaviour with Goldberg leads us to believe that she is promiscuous and superficial. However, her horror the following morning (obscurely connected with what Goldberg had in his briefcase when he entered her bedroom) shows that while she might not be especially moral she is a sexual innocent alongside Goldberg.

This brings us to the men, especially Stanley and Goldberg. The maltreatment of women by men is a theme which runs through the entire play in one form or another. It takes the form of the abuse Meg is subjected to by Stanley as well as, more disturbingly, the men's willingness to exploit women sexually, as Stanley does at the party, and Goldberg does later that night. The callous, dismissive way that Goldberg treats Lulu the morning after shows that all his charm of the preceding evening was designed with one end in mind; and that being achieved, Lulu is something to be cast aside, another victim.

Memories, truth and illusion

With the exception of Petey, all of the characters speak of the past. It is either the means by which characters define themselves to others (Goldberg, Stanley) or it is a warm refuge from the immediate pressures of life (Meg, McCann). What Pinter seems to be saying, then, is that we all need the past, or the idea of the past, at least, However, by a stroke of dramatic brilliance, he makes the past at once necessary but unverifiable. For instance, we are probably right in thinking that Goldberg's past is a fiction he creates; but we cannot be sure. In the same way, Meg's dream of a cosy bedroom and a loving father might be true, but it might not.

By this device, Pinter makes it difficult for us to pass a final judgement upon any of the characters (and therefore makes the play realistic). For instance, if Meg's dream of her childhood is true, we might feel regret that she is now living in circumstances in which she is no longer shown such devotion. However, if it is a fantasy, we feel sorry for her because her life has given her no such actual experience and she is therefore forced to invent one (perhaps to the point where she believes it to be true).

Language and comedy

For all its moods of threat and violence, *The Birthday Party* has moments of great humour. In fact, much of the humour co-exists alongside the unpleasantness. This is not to say that Pinter sanitizes the events so that they become laughable rather than threatening. The comedy of *The Birthday Party* is not of that kind. The play does not invite us into a safe, golden world of comedy in which the unpleasantness of the real world is rendered safe for our amusement. Rather, much of what we see evokes laughter and horror *simultaneously*, with the result that we are unsettled rather than comforted. The interrogation of Stanley offers an excellent example of this. For page after page he is subjected to quick-fire questioning by Goldberg and McCann. The questions – ranging from a medieval Catholic heresy, to cricket, to whether the number 846 is possible or necessary, to why the chicken crossed the road – spill out so quickly, and are so incongruous, that we find ourselves laughing at them while being uneasily aware that they are the means of reducing a man to inarticulate violence.

Comedy of a more gentle sort is apparent at the very start of the play when Pinter catches unerringly the inconsequential and unintentionally humorous patterns of cliché-ridden everyday conversation. Language between Petey and Meg exists largely to fill the silence; they have nothing much to say to each other, but feel compelled to speak because to say nothing is both rude and, if it goes on long enough, frightening. Meg's ability to state the obvious is clearly comic but also instantly recognizable as the stuff of small-talk. The exchange she and Petey have about the baby, for instance, builds to a finely judged comic anticlimax. Excited that someone has had a baby, Meg insists that Petey tell her who it was. His response that she probably will not know the woman only makes Meg more insistent. When he gives the superbly ridiculous name of the mother, Meg sadly says that she doesn't know her.

With Goldberg, Pinter uses language sometimes to comic effect, sometimes to show that, although he tries, he cannot escape his Jewish upbringing. Goldberg is given a vast range of English clichés, some cosy ('tipping his hat', giving his girlfriend 'a peck on the cheek', Uncle Barney being 'one of the old school', visits to the seaside being 'as regular as clockwork'), some vulgar (Stanley 'getting on his breasts', getting 'on everybody's wick', driving Meg 'off her conk', for instance). It is largely through Goldberg's range of clichés that Pinter dramatizes the conflicting aspects of his character (the sentimental and the vulgar) as well as arousing our suspicions about him, for he does not use them quite as ordinary native speakers do. And underneath all this runs the diction and rhythm of his background, forever revealing that try as he might to present himself as someone totally assimilated into English life, he remains a Jew. Fine examples of the way Jewish words and speech rhythms slide into his language are to be found in the speeches he makes about his wife and mother.

Structure

There are three movements to the structure of *The Birthday Party*: to begin with we are presented with an apparently trivial situation which, as it develops, becomes laden with threat, fear, danger and violence; then comes the destructive, overwhelming central action; lastly, we return to the original situation, although we see it now through different eyes as a result of what has happened. These three structural movements correspond broadly to the three acts of the play.

In the first movement, Pinter establishes the banality of the setting through Petey and Meg. When he introduces Stanley he gradually builds up the atmosphere of frustration and resentment, which merges into fear as we witness his reaction to the news that 'two gentlemen' will be arriving. The short scene between Stanley and Lulu offers some variety to the pace of the act which up till then has been leisurely in its movement. It also serves to introduce Lulu, a character Pinter will use to reveal other aspects of Stanley's and Goldberg's characters.

When Goldberg and McCann arrive, their relationship and intentions build up the suspense, partly because we find it difficult to learn anything trustworthy about them, and partly because of the way they speak of the job they have come to do. Pinter creates a gap, which he never fills, between their knowledge of why they have come, and our ignorance. He closes this act with the first explosion of violence towards which this initial movement of the play has been inevitably working and which prepares for the more extreme violence of the second movement.

Pinter constructs Act Two so that the influence of McCann and Goldberg is all-pervading in its insidiousness and menace. Stanley is subjected to a rising tide of bullying, threats, and humiliation as they seek to dominate and destroy him. The party itself becomes a grotesque parody of the freedom from normal behaviour usually associated with such occasions: Goldberg busies himself with seducing Lulu; the toast is drunk in darkness with Stanley's face eerily lit by a torch; a child's game becomes the source of violence; darkness, instead of bringing a 'safe' thrill as it would normally do at a party, unleashes further violent behaviour.

After the steady movement toward this crescendo of aggression, Pinter calms the mood in Act Three by beginning with a conversation recalling the opening situation of the play. But there is a fundamental difference between the two occasions. Now the calmness rests on the surface only; Petey is uneasy, quickly dissuading Meg from waking Stanley. Meg herself has a headache. The drum is broken, a visual reminder to us, if not to her, of the circumstances under which it happened. As the act continues, both McCann and Goldberg show signs of strain, as though they have been severely tested by what they have done. Exactly what has happened upstairs remains a disturbing mystery. Pinter denies us the comfort of knowledge, just as he does not indicate how Petey will explain Stanley's absence to Meg, or even if she will remember that he was ever there.

General questions on *The Birthday Party*

1 Compare and contrast the characters of McCann and Goldberg.

Suggested notes for essay answer:
a) *Similarities*: both capable of generating menace through speech; both 'outsiders' in terms of race and religion; both ruthless in what they do; each dependent upon the other, though in different ways.
b) *Differences*: Goldberg more suave and fluent, McCann comparatively silent and bristling; Goldberg violent in language only, McCann capable of physical violence – stronger than Goldberg; Goldberg enjoys dominating any occasion, McCann more self-effacing; Goldberg talks more about his (fictional?) past; McCann generates a cruder, more obvious, menace than Goldberg.

Remember actually to make direct comparisons and contrasts rather than offering two character studies. Look at selected incidents in detail. Give examples of Goldberg's persuasiveness with Lulu, Meg and Petey; show, by contrast, how McCann either remains silent or says little. Contrast the ways in which the two men refer to the past – Goldberg often, McCann when he drinks too much at the party. Always support your points by close reference to the play, and quote when you think it will help clarify your point.

2 What, if anything, does the play gain by being set in one room?

3 What do you learn about the characters from the dreams, memories and illusions they have?

4 If you were asked to say what you thought were the most distinctive features of *The Birthday Party* how would you answer?

5 In what ways would you say that *The Birthday Party* can be called realistic?

6 Is *The Birthday Party* weakened or strengthened as a play because we do not know why Goldberg and McCann have come for Stanley?

7 What aspects of Pinter's dramatic technique have you found most interesting in *The Birthday Party*?

8 Discuss the way in which marriage is presented.

9 Considering that Lulu makes only a few appearances, what would you say is her contribution to the play?

10 Is Meg merely a comic character?

11 How successful do you find the presentation of Goldberg?

12 'Comedy of menace.' How accurate a description of *The Birthday Party* is this?

13 Compare and contrast *The Birthday Party* with any other book you have read which includes comedy and/or violence.

14 Examine the presentation of marriage in any other book you have read.

15 With reference to a book of your choice show how the author deals with the fear of one of the characters.

The Caretaker

Act commentaries with textual notes and revision questions

Set

The entire action takes place in a single room, which indicates the narrow, confined lives the characters lead. It seems to be a lumber room, comprising a curiously ill-assorted jumble of objects, ranging from a lawn-mower to a statue of Buddha on top of a gas stove. These incongruous items illustrate the disordered, unplanned nature of the characters' lives.

Act One

Pages 7–22

Right from the start, Pinter generates our curiosity. The first character we see, Mick, leaves the room as soon as he hears voices, and he is not seen again until the end of Act 1. Immediately questions are raised. Who is he? Why is he silent for so long? Why does he leave the room?

In terms of action very little of obvious importance happens. This means that seemingly trivial details – like Davies trying on a pair of shoes, or Aston changing the plug on the toaster – take on a significance they might not otherwise have.

When Davies and Aston enter, what is immediately obvious is their shabbiness. This is hardly surprising given that Davies is a tramp, but Aston's clothing, too, is shabby and old. It gradually emerges that Davies has lost his job. As one of life's failures, he is quick to spot injustice (not being able to get a seat because they are all taken by immigrants; being expected to do jobs which are beneath his dignity), but he is also quick to declare that he has very high standards and has seen better times – his reference to having had dinner with the best, and his remarks about his wife's method of washing her underclothing, for instance. Given his unkempt appearance, both of these remarks are highly improbable, but they show how anxious he is to be thought respectable.

Aston in the mean time busies himself mending a plug, although he never makes much progress with it. It is through such a small but significant detail that Pinter shows how Aston absorbs himself in activity so that it might seem (*to him*) that he has a function in life. We notice, too, how he is kind to Davies in a variety of ways, offering him tobacco, shoes and a bed; saying that he will collect Davies's bag for him; giving him money.

When Davies asks Aston where he sleeps, we sense by his heavy hints about how windy it can be sleeping out that he is a practised scrounger who is hoping for a bed for the night. This shows us another aspect of Davies's character: although given to bursts of pride and outrage, he is at heart servile and dependent upon the kindness of others. Pinter has a fine eye for psychological realism, for Davies never misses an opportunity to provide for himself. This is evident not only in his concern about somewhere to sleep and shoes, but in more incidental details, such as when Aston offers him some tobacco. As it is cigarette tobacco, Davies at first refuses, saying that he doesn't smoke cigarettes. Almost immediately, however, he declares he will have some for his pipe.

Davies' long and unintentionally amusing account of his journey to the monastery is one of the comic highlights of this act, but it also reveals his ingratitude. The incident which follows, in which he tries on a pair of shoes, praises them highly, only to deflate Aston by saying that they are too small, reveals his contradictory nature. In the previous paragraph, we saw how he is always alert to what might benefit him. However, he also needs to see himself as proud and discerning – for example, he speaks knowledgeably of the merits of leather against suede to impress Aston before he rejects the shoes. Pinter uses this incident with the shoes to illustrate that although Davies is a servile old tramp he is also a human being who needs to maintain some shreds of self-respect.

Davies's sudden declaration that he must get to Sidcup takes us as much by surprise as it does Aston. Sidcup is not far from London where Davies is at present and so he could easily get there if he really wanted to. More importantly, it is one of those ordinary places which Pinter invests with comic meaning in his plays. (He has just done the same with Luton.) Because Sidcup is an unremarkable, middle-class town, Davies's passionate desire to get there, as though it is a place of pilgrimage, is at once comic and inappropriate. As the action of the play develops, so does the importance of Sidcup. Davies is rootless, aimless and without a clear sense of who he is; his wish to get to Sidcup is merely a dream, a pathetic aspiration, something to give him hope for the future and a sense of purpose.

Paralleling Davies's dream of getting to Sidcup is Aston's dream of building a shed in the garden (and, later in the play, Mick's dream of converting the room into a luxury penthouse apartment). Aston's dream, too, is unlikely ever to be fulfilled, but it gives his life a sense of purpose. The way in which dreams and hopes govern us and give meaning and purpose to our lives is an important theme in the play. Pinter evokes an ambiguous response from us here (and elsewhere) in the play with regard to this matter. While the relatively unambitious nature of the Aston and Davies's hopes makes us pity them, the importance of dreams in their lives is not questioned. Pinter at once makes fun of the drabness of their ambition, and at the same time understands the pathos in the situation.

The filthy skate, an old man like me Davies curses the man for bullying an old man like him.

'I've had dinner with the best Unlikely to be true, but notice how anxious Davies is to show that he has known better times.

git Idiot.

Anyway, I'm obliged to you ... You got any more rooms then, have you? Read this page carefully and you will see how Davies is already angling for somewhere to spend the night.

This is your house then, is it? ... I thought there must be someone living there. Look at the speeches between these two pieces of dialogue. They are an excellent example of the way Pinter captures the circular, repetitive movement of ordinary conversation.

S⸜epherd's Bush When Pinter wrote the play, this was an unfashionable area in London, the kind of place that a tramp like Davies would frequent.

convenience Public lavatory. As with all of Davies' feeble attempts to impress Aston, this speech reveals a great deal about the sordidness of his life. However, although *we* see it as illustrating Davies' shabbiness, *he* regards the man who worked in the public lavatory as an example of the successful friends he has.

Can't wear shoes that don't fit ... all the good's gone out of them Davies's account of what happened at the monastery is one of the comic highpoints of Act One. Not only is there the highly improbable vulgarity of the monk, but also Davies's suggestion that the monks are ruled by a mother superior (chief nun in a convent). The story not only shows Davies' ingratitude; it also shows how his memory distorts the event. Pinter creates doubt in our minds by making us uncertain how to respond to Davies's stories about his past. He might be lying, or misremembering.

What do you do for a cup of tea? ... That's a bit rough. Note how quickly he moves from gratitude at being given somewhere to sleep to criticism of the facilities offered.

Buddha 'The Enlightened.' Buddhism is a religious system of eastern Asia. Having a figure representing 'the Enlightened' in a play in which the characters are so unenlightened is ironic. Note, too, that Aston bought the statue because he liked the look of it. While he might not be religious, there is a side to him that responds to the calm, reassuring figure of the Buddha.

Oh, they're . . . en't they? Aston's question takes Davies by surprise. He probably has no idea what a Buddha is and so makes this unintentionally comic reply.

papers We never know exactly what papers he means, just as we never learn if they actually exist, but to Davies they are the means of establishing his identity.

Insurance card National Insurance. People in employment pay part of their income to ensure that they qualify for a state pension, unemployment pay, and so on. Payments are recorded by stamps being stuck onto an insurance card. The one he produces could have been found lying about.

Pages 22–27

Next morning, Aston remarks that Davies seemed to be having nightmares, which might have been caused by his sleeping in a strange bed. Davies becomes defensive. Always frightened of being revealed for the failure he is, he misunderstands Aston, and asserts that he has slept in plenty of beds. He quickly puts the blame for the noise on the Blacks. Three of his most enduring characteristics are displayed here: the speed with which he takes offence, his racism, and his willingness to blame anybody but himself.

When Davies sees Aston preparing to go out, he instantly rushes to join him. His surprise at being allowed to stay in the house during Aston's absence gives another important insight into his character; it reveals how little he has been trusted in the past. Aston recounts an odd experience he had in a café when a woman asked if she could have a look at his body. This is unlikely enough in itself, but in a superbly comic moment Pinter has Davies top this by claiming several women have said the same thing to him. His wish to appear as a desirable man of the world is amusing, but also shows us clearly that he has no idea of how far short he falls of that standard. After his momentary boast, his underlying uncertainty is exposed again in three ways: when Aston asks him where he was born; when he shows his fear of electricity; and when he believes that the cooker can gas him even though it is not connected. Davies's reluctance to answer Aston's innocent question creates ambiguity. It is possible, given his aimless style of life, that he has genuinely forgotten; it is equally possible that questions about his background make him suspicious (they are the kinds of questions people in authority ask) and so he is deliberately evasive. By refusing to give us a definite answer, Pinter makes the play like real life; there are countless occasions when we cannot know for sure the real reason why people say what they do. In the second and third instances, Pinter shows how remote Davies is from what most people consider to be basic aspects of modern life.

Eh, mister, just one thing . . . you know? Davies might have forgotten that he has already asked Aston for money, or, recognizing a soft-hearted person, he could be trying his luck again.

might get down to Wembley later in the day An area of north London not far from where the play is set (with a huge stadium). Davies does not actually go there. Like his intention of going to Sidcup, he has set himself an objective he will never realize.

Pages 27–29

The short, final section of the act is an explosion of unexpected violence. It is worth noting how unexpectedly Pinter springs it upon us. By doing so he shows the very real danger of the world Davies inhabits (a tramp is likely to find himself the victim of sudden attack). He also defines central features of Mick's character even before he speaks: his ability to dominate and frighten; his swift, decisive physical actions (contrast Aston); his enjoyment of violence.

Much of this act has shown Davies as a victim, either real or imagined: of ethnic minorities; of bullying superiors; of vicious monks; even of the weather which will not allow him to get to Sidcup. Now, having for once been trusted by someone, he suddenly becomes the victim of a bully. From being a haven of peace and quiet, the room suddenly becomes a trap. Notice that Mick's final position, sitting in silence, takes us back to the start of the play. By the clever device of showing him in the room at the beginning, Pinter, as well as rousing our curiosity, has established in our minds that he is in some way associated with it. In Act Two he begins to develop that association.

Revision questions and assignments on Act One

1 Make a list of the main points of Aston's character as they strike you in this act.

2 Write a character study of Davies, basing your answer upon: his racism; his story of the monks near Luton; his story about Sidcup; the noises he makes when he sleeps.

3 By referring to one or two particular instances in the act, show how Pinter catches the repetitive, humdrum nature of much conversation.

4 Nothing much actually happens in this act. How does Pinter stop us from becoming bored?

Act Two

Pages 30–36

Mick dominates this section (note the length of his three uninterrupted speeches). He is threatening from the start, using pauses and repetitions to make Davies feel uneasy. The way he repeats the name 'Jenkins' is an excellent illustration of the undefined but very real menace he generates. Davies cannot be sure of Mick's reason for repeating his name. Does he do it because he finds it amusing, or because he does not believe it is Davies' real name, or because he is mocking him? Then, with an abrupt change of attitude, Mick becomes very polite, telling Davies how glad he is to meet him, only to re-adopt moments later a more menacing line of enquiry before launching into a long speech which becomes more preposterous as it goes on.

This establishes the pattern for the entire section, with Mick sometimes threatening physical violence, sometimes speaking at great length about events which seem unlikely in the extreme, and sometimes using short, clipped questions as a means of interrogating Davies. At the start, Mick's behaviour seems to raise more questions than it answers. In his long speeches, for instance, is he merely hoping to disorientate Davies by a barrage of nonsense in order to get at the truth? Or does he actually believe it all himself? Is he sane or mad? As the act develops, we come to doubt that he is mad. Rather, we see him as an accomplished sadist whose mercurial changes of tone of voice, length and topic of conversation, and masterly ability to strike Davies where he is weakest, must eventually break Davies down.

The speech in which Mick offers to sell the house to Davies shows his genius for attacking him where he is weakest. It is blatantly obvious from Davies's appearance that he is in no position to consider buying a house. Mick's speech is therefore both mocking and menacing. We have already seen in Act One how ignorant – and frightened – Davies is of everyday things like gas and electricity. How much more will he be frightened by all the financial and legal jargon that Mick hurls at him.

A drip sounds in the bucket overhead. Pinter uses this sound to create an atmosphere of dramatic tension before Mick launches into his speech. As dripping water is associated with torture, it underlines Mick's intention to frighten Davies.

You remind me of my uncle's brother ... went to Jamaica Notice how the rapid changes of subject, together with the short, urgent sentences are all the more effective after the succession of pauses.

Used to go in number four for Beckenham Reserves Mick mixes cricket and football imagery here in order to confuse Davies. In cricket, batsman number 4 goes in at the fall of the second wicket.

papoose American Indian baby.

You know, believe it or not ... there was nothing in it As with his first long speech, this one shows Mick's mania for detail. All the places he names actually exist, but more importantly the sheer volume of detail is meant to confuse Davies.

I got the bullet I lost my job.

family allowances A state allowance, which a parent is entitled to have for each child.

No strings attached ... double check. What each of these details means is less important than the cumulatively bewildering effect they would have upon Davies. As a tramp he would, of course, not own shares, or even have a bank account.

Pages 36–39

In this short section, Aston comes back. The repetitive conversation between Mick and himself about how to stop the leak offers another fine example of Pinter's ability to capture the banality of ordinary conversation. Aston's announcement that he has brought back Davies' bag is further evidence of his thoughtfulness. Mick's menacing/mocking attitude to Davies is apparent in the way he snatches it.

What follows is an extended series of stage directions which choreograph a sequence of movements with all the precision of a ballet. The intention is clearly humorous, as the bag passes to and fro between Davies, Mick and Aston, but there is still the undercurrent of threat from Mick who is responsible for what happens. In this incident we see Davies once more as the victim, Mick as the unpredictable aggressor, and Aston as neutral. Once again, Pinter makes use of the drip in the bucket, this time not so much to provide a moment of dramatic tension as to signal a change from choreographed movement back to speech; after the incident with the bag, there is a pause, the drip of water into the bucket at which they all look, another pause, and then speech.

What do you do . . . when that bucket's full? The abruptness of
Davies's first comment leads us to expect a much more significant
question, but, as if over-awed by having Aston and Mick stare at him,
he lapses into banality. Aston's reply, after a pause, that they empty it
is nicely humorous in its inevitability. What else does one do with a full
bucket?

sonny Mick's calling Davies, who is an old man, 'son' and 'sonny' are
clearly insulting.

Pages 39–44

Immediately after the departure of Mick, Davies and Aston engage in another circular conversation, this time about Mick's sense of humour. Davies, who is bewildered and frightened by Mick's behaviour, asks tentatively if he is a joker. Aston answers positively that he is. Moments later, Davies triumphantly uses Aston's exact words as though to explain to Aston (who identified the matter in the first place!) that Mick has got a sense of humour.

As Aston puts the statue of Buddha on the gas stove (thereby revealing how the spiritual and material are jumbled in his mind), he tells Davies that he is refurbishing the room for Mick whose house it is. This is an important piece of information for Davies which will affect his attitude toward both Mick and Aston. He knows now that ownership – and therefore power –

are lodged with Mick, not with his brother. In order to secure his own future in the house, therefore, Mick needs to be cultivated at the expense of Aston.

Aston's long speech about the shed he wants to build in the garden (his longest speech so far) reveals a deep, obscure yearning in him, and links up with Davies' wish to go to Sidcup and Mick's desire to make the apartment luxurious. In all three cases, there is the suggestion that what is important is not the achievement of the dream, but the consolation and hope that are to be found in having one. What makes Aston, like Davies, so sad and pathetic a character is the smallness of his dream.

Davies's discovery that the bag Aston has brought back is not his after all reveals two important points. Firstly, Davies's suspicious nature; his assumption that 'they' have kept his bag shows how threatening he feels the world to be. This aspect of his character is developed later in the section when Aston offers him a job as caretaker. Secondly, the fact that it is the wrong bag shows that although Aston is well intentioned he is utterly ineffectual.

When Aston offers Davies the job of caretaker, Pinter creates a wonderful piece of comic dialogue in which both of them mutter broken, incoherent phrases, and meaningless clichés. In everyday speech, vocabulary is often limited and inadequate; people rely on tone of voice and gesture to convey their meaning.

The humour of the situation continues when Pinter has Davies self-importantly announce that such a job would need implements; he clearly thinks that this word sounds technical and is therefore connected with special expertise. Pinter mocks Davies here, but shows, too, how he craves status. It is both pathetic and comic that the symbols Davies associates with such prestige, an overall and a broom, are so mundane. However, Aston's proposal falls flat when he suggests that they could fit a bell with a sign saying 'Caretaker' outside the front door. Immediately Davies becomes defensive. His long, closing speech about what 'they' would do if they found him demonstrates his fear and vulnerability.

He's got a sense of humour This is another example of the way in which Pinter can give a menacing edge to a remark which on the surface is bland.

He's a real joker, that lad Thinking back over what Mick has done to him, Davies's sarcastic comment shows how frightened of Mick he is.

No, what I need is a kind of shirt ... with stripes going down. Davies's assumption that only striped shirts can be warm is highly comic, but it also serves to show how illogical people can be. Moments after having declined the shirts (which are useful) Davies accepts the smoking-jacket which has little practical use at all, although, because it is associated with the rich and socially well-established, it satisfies his vanity.

any Harry Any Tom, Dick or Harry.

Pages 44–52

This section opens with Davies being threatened, or thinking he is being threatened, by someone in the darkened room. When the light comes on, Mick is revealed holding the vacuum cleaner. He tells Davies that he had to plug it into the light socket. This seems a satisfactory explanation, except that we remember Davies's box of matches being kicked away and the nozzle of the cleaner moving along the floor after him, causing him to fall. Pinter creates uncertainty in our minds (and in Davies's too). We have no way of knowing if these incidents were accidental or intentional, but they serve to strengthen the idea of Mick being a person who enjoys victimizing others.

However, when he and Davies talk, they seem to establish a more cordial relationship. When Mick expresses admiration for Davies's courage, Davies softens and even takes the sandwich Mick offers him. They discuss Aston, Mick commenting that his brother is lazy. Davies's reply that he knows all about that sort of person is very ironic as he is 'that sort of person' himself. This confidential note marks a new and important development in the relationship between Davies and Mick. We notice as their conversation progresses how quickly Davies sides with Mick (who has treated him so far with little regard) and criticizes Aston (who has shown him kindness). We remember, also, that Davies knows the house belongs to Mick and we begin to suspect that Davies is moving allegiance from one brother to the other, more powerful, one. However, Mick seems to sense Davies's willingness to betray Aston and warns him not to be too critical. This sudden change of attitude throws Davies on the defensive once more, and is another example of the way Mick dominates Davies by his unpredictability.

   Mick's offer to Davies of the job as caretaker parallels the offer
Aston has already made, but Davies, anxious to ingratiate himself with Mick, makes no mention of the earlier offer. Mick's
wish to see references promises to be a problem for Davies, who
mentions having plenty of references in Sidcup (something
which seems unlikely). Mick's remark that they can always get his
references if they want them is one of those powerfully ambiguous, vaguely menacing remarks which are a feature of Pinter's
style. On the surface Mick is simply being prudent, but there is
the implication that there will be trouble for Davies if he cannot
get hold of them. At the close, Davies returns to something
dearer to his heart than a job – he asks Mick about a pair of
shoes.

I'm sorry if I gave you a start ... that's all. Mick's concern for Davies's
   welfare takes us by surprise. His politeness makes it difficult for Davies
   to be sure if he is being sincere or sarcastic.
**I mean, you're my brother's friend, aren't you ... I'm sorry to hear my
   brother's not very friendly.** Note how easily Mick distorts the
   meaning of Davies's remark. Davies, frightened of committing himself
   to saying that Aston is friendly, dithers, and therefore allows Mick to
   menace him.
Well he's a funny bloke, your brother ... Nothing. Once more Mick
   deliberately misinterprets what Davies says. Davies means funny in the
   sense of strange; Mick interprets it in the sense of amusing.
in the services ... I was one of the first over there Davies's replies
   show that he is lying to impress Mick. The idea of the disorganized
   Davies having spent half his life in the armed forces is ridiculous.

Pages 52–54

Davies and Aston both slept badly. Notice how Davies, once so
grateful for a bed to sleep in, now complains bitterly about the
draught from the window. Notice, too, how he reminds Aston of
his need of a pair of shoes. He has moved from being grateful
for what he has been given to *expecting* special treatment.

Ay, well, that's shot it, en't it? That's put paid to that idea. The speed
   with which Davies decides that he cannot go to Sidcup because of the
   weather suggests his relief that the decision has been made for him.

Pages 54–57

In the longest speech of the play, Aston reflects upon how he came to receive brain treatment in a hospital. Electrodes were placed on his head and electrical currents sent through his brain. This had the effect of making him docile, but clearly has tampered with him as a human being. (In this he is like Alex in *A Clockwork Orange*, the novel by Anthony Burgess.) He cannot clearly remember why he was admitted – in this respect the operation has robbed him of his past and therefore of a large part of his identity. He seems to think it was because he talked too much. As the speech develops, it becomes an increasingly poignant account of how, through a sinister process, he was rendered 'safe' to be returned to society. He seems to believe that the people in the factory and the café were somehow responsible for what happened to him; hence his subsequent avoidance of such places. The speech stands as a criticism of an uncaring society which likes conformity and material success and has little time for those who are ill. His wish to build a shed is a pathetic desire on his part to satisfy the creative urge all human beings have. Pinter suggests through Aston here that everyone needs a purpose in life in order to give it some shape and order.

minor Someone under the legal age of adulthood; at the time the play was written this was 21.

Revision questions and assignments on Act Two

1 Imagine that you are Mick. Try to account for the way in which you treat Davies in Act Two.

2 Using information only from this act, show how Mick and Aston differ as characters.

3 What evidence is there in this act that Davies is becoming dissatisfied with Aston?

4 Read Aston's final speech very carefully. What do we learn of Aston through it?

5 By carefully selecting relevant details in this act, show how Pinter creates an atmosphere of menace.

6 What do you find comic in this act?

Act Three

Pages 58–64

In this section Davies becomes much more voluble. This reflects the way his confidence has grown now that he has somewhere to live and a degree of respect from Mick. The complaints he directs against Aston reveal both his ingratitude and his increasing awareness of what he considers to be his due. It seems that everything Aston does is wrong: he has failed to give Davies a bread knife; he has left the gas stove in the room; he has little to say for himself. We notice how cunningly Davies attempts to drive a wedge between Aston and Mick. The pause at the end of his long speech, just before he mentions that he and Mick could make a success of the flat together, hints very strongly that Davies has been giving careful thought to ousting Aston altogether.

Mick's description of how the flat might be decorated clearly persuades Davies that his plan is succeeding, but once again Mick takes Davies by surprise when he remarks that he and Aston would live there. Davies is not deterred, however. He launches into another lengthy criticism of Aston, this time about Aston's failure to supply him with a clock. He associates clocks and timekeeping with conventional, orderly life and business from which he has been excluded; that is why he wants one. The only *reason* he can give for wanting one is that he will then know when to have a cup of tea!

Having exhausted his complaints about the clock, he bends closer to Mick and comes as near as he dares to suggesting that he and Mick should work together to the exclusion of Aston. Idle though he is, he even offers to decorate the room.

DAVIES *is sitting in the chair . . . smoking jacket* Occupying the prominent position in the room and wearing the jacket he would associate with the rich, respectable classes, Davies clearly sees himself now as a man of some importance, a pathetic delusion.

I got a knife . . . No, what I want— A revealing example of how Davies' expectations have risen. When he first appears he is grateful for some cigarette tobacco for his pipe; now he feels he cannot be expected to cut bread without the proper kind of knife.

What about this gas stove? . . . conversation with you In this litany of complaints, note how often the words 'I' and 'me' appear, revealing Davies's selfishness.

he don't care about me An instance of Davies's selfishness; ironic given that he shows so little concern for Aston.

penthouse A flat, often luxurious and exclusive, on the top floor of a high building.

afromosia A wood from the west coast of Africa used as an alternative to teak, which is a very expensive hardwood.

Clobber Rubbish

Tchaikovsky A Russian composer (1840–93); his work is still very popular. By inviting Davies round for drink and the chance to listen to some classical music, Mick is once more making fun of him.

Pages 64–66

Ironically, given Davies's earlier scathing remarks about him, Aston enters with a pair of shoes, something Davies has wanted since the outset of the play. Instead of being grateful, Davies is critical. First of all, he complains that they do not fit properly; then, he grudgingly concedes that they are just about bearable until he manages to get another pair; then, he disapproves strongly of the brown laces Aston finds him for the black shoes. Again, we notice here how he expects Aston to do everything for him (he has done nothing to secure himself a pair of shoes) and how his expectations have risen.

His boast that he has been offered a good job (by Mick) degenerates into self-absorbed complaining, so that he does not even notice Aston depart. When he does notice that he is alone, his response is typically critical of Aston.

Pages 66–70

The relationship between Aston and Davies deteriorates noticeably in this section and finally breaks down altogether. First, Davies' anger at being roused by Aston because of the noise he is making results in Davies making a lengthy and very angry speech. It brings together several unpleasant strands in Davies' character which have been present throughout the play but which Pinter has been deepening and intensifying as the action progresses. He complains about the coldness of the room, tries to alarm Aston by telling him that Mick is dissatisfied with him, and then, in the most cruel attack of all, resorts to crude insults about the treatment Aston received in hospital, taking a malicious pleasure in suggesting that Aston is a lunatic. It is a clear case of the victim turned victimizer.

However, it soon becomes evident that Davies's new-found confidence is very fragile. When Aston, not unnaturally, makes a slight move toward him, Davies over-reacts, producing his knife. A quarrel starts, but it is Aston's accusation that Davies smells which provokes the strongest reaction. Davies, outraged by the suggestion, actually thrusts at Aston with his knife (one of his few assertive actions in the play) but stops short of actually wounding him. After this climax, Davies's courage deserts him. When Aston tells him to leave, his responses are snivelling and childlike. He does as he is told and departs.

If you wouldn't keep mucking ... no noises! Notice that Davies says it is Aston's fault for the noises he (Davies) makes while sleeping.
It's getting so freezing in here ... that before in my life. Given that Davies is a tramp, this is highly unlikely.
a creamer A lunatic.

Pages 70–74

Davies returns with Mick, still outraged that Aston has said he stinks. One of the things that makes Davies such a credible character is that he is more annoyed at being insulted in this way than he is worried at the prospect of losing somewhere to sleep. Once more we notice that, although Mick at first seems to be sympathetic, he unsettles Davies by asking him what he means when he says that Aston has no sense. Immediately Davies starts hedging. Mick seems to be toying with Davies, enjoying the confusion he creates by his abrupt changes of attitude. A little later, he takes Davies completely by surprise when he assumes that he is a skilled interior decorator. Davies has never claimed to be any such thing and protests, making Mick angry.

In his frustration, Davies refers to Aston as 'nutty'. Mick suddenly springs to his brother's defence. At first he circles Davies, insulting him and finally telling him to go. Then, as his anger mounts, he hurls the Buddha against the stove, breaking it. This seems strange, as the Buddha was greatly valued by Aston whom Mick has just been defending. As well as showing how unpredictable and dangerous he can be, the smashing of the Buddha reveals that Mick lacks Aston's liking for serene, even spiritual, objects. As though this action has precipitated a private crisis in Mick's own mind, in his next speech he expresses his frustration with Aston.

What? What I'm saying is . . . we can both see him for what he is. Davies realizes he has been unwise in mentioning Aston's illness and rapidly backtracks, hoping to ingratiate himself with Mick.

What did you call my brother? Mick's use of the phrase 'my brother' shows how, despite everything, the bond between himself and Aston is stronger than any other.

What a strange man you are . . . Here's half a dollar. A great deal of Mick's speech is as applicable to himself as it is to Davies, especially his references to Davies being violent, erratic and unpredictable.

half a dollar A half-crown or 2/6, equivalent to about 12p, but worth much more when the play was written.

Pages 75–78

Aston enters the room and faces Mick. Their shared smiles suggest a bond. Mick leaves, Aston busies himself with mending a plug, and Davies begins self-consciously to explain why he is in the room after Aston had asked him to leave. Davies's tone is wheedling and ingratiating as he tries to persuade Aston to allow him to stay. He suggests they change beds to overcome the problem of the draught, but Aston is unwilling. Davies even offers to build the shed for Aston, again only to be refused. As Davies begins to realize that he will definitely have to leave, he becomes more desperate. All his self-importance has vanished. The play closes with his pathetic suggestion that perhaps he might be allowed to stay if he gets his papers from Sidcup. His speech tails away, uncompleted.

Revision questions and assignments on Act Three

1 By selecting a few relevant details, show how Pinter presents the increasing ingratitude of Davies towards Aston.

2 Choose two or three occasions in the act when Pinter creates a sense of menace and try to account for how it is done.

3 How successful do you find the ending of the play?

4 Write a brief essay in which you discuss Pinter's use of pauses in this act.

Pinter's art in *The Caretaker*
Characters

Davies

'I never had a dream in my life.'

Davies is the most important character in the play, on stage for virtually the duration of the action. His appearance is unattractive: he is a shabbily dressed, dirty tramp, and both Mick and Aston accuse him of smelling, something to which he takes great exception. Pinter builds his character from a few recurring features, as he does with Mick and Aston.

In Davies, Pinter presents unsentimentally a total failure. While he makes him entirely credible, he also suggests through him certain elemental human characteristics. We might not like Davies very much, but we often see rather unpleasant shades of ourselves in what he says and does, in his ingratitude, perpetual dissatisfaction, boastfulness and selfishness, for instance.

Lonely and alone, Davies trusts no one. For him, the world outside the room is a dangerous and incomprehensible place. It is a place of nights spent with nowhere to sleep, of temporary, menial jobs, of not having enough to eat, of walking from London to Luton in the hope of begging a pair of shoes. He is frightened of having a sign saying 'caretaker' fixed to the front door in case representatives of authority come demanding to check his insurance card. Even in the relative security of the room there is danger. Appliances such as electric switches, cookers and vacuum cleaners frighten him. Yet when he is left alone in the room at the end of Act One, he shows all the wonderment and curiosity of a child, making it clear to us that being alone in a room is a new experience for him.

Davies's identity is always in doubt. Some of the stories he tells, such as having served in the colonies, are clearly lies; others, such as his walk to the monastery in Luton, might be true. He claims that his real name is Mac Davies, and Bernard Jenkins is an assumed one, though why he should want to assume a name is not clear. Even the insurance card he takes from his pocket need not necessarily be his. Most of us take our identity for granted, but for someone in Davies's position, with no settled way of life, the need to be able to establish an identity can be crucial. That is why Sidcup features so largely; it gives him the illusion that his identity – and therefore his security and his place in society – are there waiting for him. He will never actually go there because it seems unlikely that there are any papers and he does not wish to face up to that reality. But his delusion that he can if necessary prove who he is allows him to drift on in his aimless way.

Pinter establishes quickly the sense of grievance Davies has against the world. Blacks, Poles, Greeks, employers, his wife (if he ever had one) are all criticized within minutes of his appearance. We quickly begin to suspect that one of the ways in which Davies comes to terms with his own failure is by blaming it upon others. This sense of grievance is something that Pinter develops throughout the play. At first, Davies is grateful to Aston for allowing him a bed, but he soon finds reason for complaint – the open window causes a draught and there is no clock in the room. It is as though Pinter is revealing the ease with which we attach blame to others rather than looking to ourselves to explain our predicament. Immigrants, of course, provide Davies with a wonderful opportunity to evade the responsibility for his own failure. His racism is objectionable but the reason for it is clear enough. A failure among his own countrymen, Davies is still 'English' and as such feels superior to those who are not.

Allied to Davies's sense of grievance is his attempt at self-esteem. Clearly one of life's casualties, rootless, penniless and without importance, he is quick to state that he has known better times. The remark early in Act One that he has had dinner with the best, and his quickness to assert later in the same Act that he has slept in plenty of beds, are feeble attempts to convince Aston of things which are obviously untrue. In fact his very need to make such comments reinforces for us how untrue they are. This can lead to comedy on occasions, as when he declares that women have often desired him. The improbability of this is reinforced in performance when one can actually see Davies for the shabby, dirty character he is.

An abject failure, Davies, in a very human way, craves respect. Yet the perilous nature of his existence means that he cannot afford to turn down the chance to beg. So he is deferential to Aston to begin with and begs shoes and money from him. Towards the close of the play, as we have seen, even the mild-mannered Aston can reduce Davies to grovelling. Stripped of all self-respect, he expresses interest in the plug Aston has been poking at, confesses that he made noises whilst asleep, and even says that he is willing to betray Mick and be Aston's man. The interplay of these two characteristics, self-esteem and servility, is one of the great strengths of Pinter's presentation because it means that our response to Davies is never static. We are either irritated or amused by his boasting, or moved by the pathos of his begging.

One of Davies' least likeable characteristics is his selfishness. Although he complains bitterly that he has been the victim of others' selfishness, Davies is equally selfish given the chance. Pinter seems to be hinting at the deeply ingrained and very unpleasant ways in which human beings abuse power. Given the opportunity, victims of the abuse of power become victimizers. This is shown clearly in the way Davies betrays Aston. As we have seen, Aston shows Davies nothing but kindness. Instead of being thankful, Davies tries to create a split between the two brothers, to oust Aston and form a partnership with Mick. This is most evident in Act Three when dressed in his smoking jacket and holding his pipe, Davies thinks he has established a dominant position in the room. Confident now, he launches into a series of criticisms of Aston, never thinking that perhaps Mick is allowing him enough rope to hang himself. Later, when asked by Aston to leave, he declares that Aston is the one who should go.

Deciding how to respond to Davies is difficult, and this is a measure of Pinter's success in creating him. We are shown quite unsparingly how unpleasant Davies is. He is idle, violent, selfish, racist, complaining and disloyal. Pinter has caught unerringly in his speech patterns and language his concern with survival. Yet to dismiss Davies in this way is quite inadequate, for there are times when he wins our sympathy. In one sense he deserves to be cast back out onto the street, and yet his pleading at the end of the play is so devoid of dignity and so despairing that we pity him as we would an animal. There exists a tension between our wish to judge him morally and our wish to feel compassion for him. We cannot systematize our response, and this is what makes Davies such a memorable character.

Mick

'I could turn this place into a penthouse'

It is difficult to know what Mick is thinking and what his motives are. When we see him at the start of the play, staring in turn at each object in the room and then leaving when he hears voices, we assume that what he is doing is significant in some way, but we do not know why. He begins by being a series of gestures which do not add up to a personality.

On his second appearance at the end of Act One, the violent streak in his nature is revealed. He has no idea who Davies is, of course, and he could be protecting his property from a would-be burglar. But Pinter implies that there is more to it than this. There is for one thing the silent menace with which Mick moves; then he deals quickly and efficiently with Davies; then, not content with this, he pushes Davies back down with his foot and stands over him. All this without saying a word.

When he does speak to Davies, he displays great skill in confusing him. The pleasure he gains from unsettling Davies is clearly part of his sadistic nature. He begins Act Two, for instance, by interrogating Davies in a clipped manner, repeating his name, and using pauses to sinister effect. Then, in a parody of good manners, he says how awfully nice it is to meet him. A little later he launches into the first of a series of long speeches about Davies' appearance, which become more and more preposterous as they go on. The inconsistency of his attitude irritates Davies, but is Mick's way of getting power over him. He baffles Davies, threatens him, appears concerned that he slept well, and then taunts him by flicking his trousers in his face.

One thing we notice about Mick is his fluency. A good example is the speech in which he begins by telling Davies that he smells. It is quite obvious from Davies's appearance that he is little better than a tramp, but Mick goes through a funny, though cruel, routine in which he offers Davies a series of deals involving solicitors, decorators, insurance, a personal medical attendant and a bank, all of which are totally outside Davies' experience. His cruel mocking nature is presented to us without any explanation or justification.

The speech he makes in Act Three about wanting to turn the room into a penthouse is clearly important. In its expensive, though rather vulgar, decoration and furnishings, the penthouse would present a marked contrast to the shabbiness of the room, littered with Aston's rubbish. Yet Mick's dream is of sharing the flat with Aston, suggesting the depth of the bond between them. Moments later, though, Mick criticizes Aston for having no interest in his dreams. The relationship between the two brothers, though deep, is complex and contradictory. This is not to be seen as a dramatic weakness in Pinter. Rather, it shows his concern with portraying the way in which resentments and tensions compete with loyalty and love in human relationships.

Aston

'I want to build that shed out in the garden'

There seems to be an odd discrepancy between what Aston wears and what he does. The dark-blue pin-stripe suit is a symbol of the conventional businessman, yet he seems to be some kind of builder, forever fiddling with electric plugs and dreaming of building a shed, but never getting very far with either. Perhaps the suit represents the way in which he has been made 'safe' by his treatment in the hospital, and rendered fit to be a respectable member of society. By giving us only Aston's words to guide us, Pinter makes it deliberately unclear why Aston was operated on. The point is that even when Aston tries to describe something central to his life, he cannot communicate it precisely.

One of his most obvious features is his generosity. In this he provides a marked contrast to his brother. He offers Davies shelter, money, employment and clothing. However, his very kindness leaves him vulnerable to attacks from Davies. It is ironic that Davies speaks to Aston, who is kind to him, in a way he would never dare speak to Mick, who taunts and torments him.

Aston tells Davies in Act One that he likes working with his hands, but for all his talk of building the shed and for all his working with electric plugs, he accomplishes very little in the play. His busyness appears to be an excuse for getting nothing done rather than a means of attaining targets. By keeping himself preoccupied, Aston manages to give his life some sense of purpose, although this leads Mick to complain that Aston is hopeless as a workman. What Pinter shows very powerfully through Aston is a mind rendered too timid to confront those issues with which it is faced. It has been rendered so by a society which dislikes misfits and tampers with their brains to make them 'safe'. One of the things we learn from Aston's long speech is that the world outside the room is hostile. Unable to give his life much drive or direction, Aston instead takes refuge in dreams and pointless fiddling with plugs.

Pinter shows the disordered state of Aston's mind in several ways. Perhaps most obviously, there is the room itself which, with its clutter of ill-assorted objects, serves as a visual symbol of Aston's cluttered brain. Aston's manner of speaking, too, is revealing. Much of the time, his speeches are short, as though the difficulty of formulating thoughts and expressing them is almost too much for him. When he does speak at greater length, it is usually significant in terms of the presentation of his character. Three examples will help show this. Firstly, in Act One, there are the occasions when he tells Davies about the time he ordered a Guinness in a pub and later when he describes the occasion when the woman talked to him in the café. Both occurrences are important to Aston, but what we remember most about them is their oddity. For one thing, they are quite unconnected with what has been said previously and, having introduced the topics, Aston is unable to develop them into further conversation. They exist as vivid but unconnected fragments. What we get is a glimpse of a disordered mind lost in its own thoughts and only half aware of what is going on outside it.

The second example occurs in Act Two when Aston tells Davies about the shed he intends building. In his musing about the shed and then the room, Aston seems to forget Davies's presence. In this way, and through the hesitant, broken phrases he uses, Pinter reveals the extent to which dreaming gives Aston some sense of purpose.

The third instance is Aston's long speech at the end of Act Two. As with so much of the play, we can never actually be sure that what Aston tells us is completely true, but its sheer length and irregular rhythms show a mind under great stress. Aston depicts himself as a helpless victim, betrayed not only by an uncaring society, but also by his mother who gave permission for the operation to be performed. Although the speech sensationalizes the brutality of the treatment, it dramatizes powerfully the traumatic effect it had upon Aston, making him both timid, cautious, and frightened of people. This last point makes his kindness to Davies all the more remarkable.

Yet although Aston is kind, he does finally have the determination to ask Davies to leave. He does this only after Davies has been particularly offensive, and then in a mild manner, even offering Davies some money to get to Sidcup. It is only when Davies speaks dismissively of the shed that Aston becomes angry. He can take insult after insult; what he cannot endure is having anyone speak disrespectfully of the dream that gives his life a semblance of purpose.

Themes

See p. 36 for general note on Pinter themes.

Violence and menace/the Outsider

Pinter is a master at creating a dramatic world in which violence and menace lurk just below the surface. In Mick, for instance, Pinter shows someone who finds pleasure in frightening others. His movements on stage are often swift and silent, he is unpredictable in his behaviour, subjecting Davies to physical violence at first and then to more subtle but very unsettling exhibitions of verbal menace. Davies is never quite sure where he stands with him. Yet it is possible also to see Davies as presenting a menace to Mick, a threat to his relationship with Aston. After all, it is Aston who invited Davies in. Although Mick complains to Davies about Aston being lazy, at the end the bond between the two brothers is shown to be stronger than that between either of them and Davies, the outsider.

Violence and menace figure largely in Aston's life, too, although unlike Mick he is always the victim and never the perpetrator. His description of the pincers being put on his skull in the hospital shocks us, largely because one associates hospitals with easing pain rather than causing it. What is important is that, for him, the world beyond the room has become dangerous and threatening. People who do not behave in the way society accepts are taken away and made 'safe', even if this means rendering them timid and frightened of the world at large.

The most obvious source of menace is Mick. Davies is not only the victim of physical assault, but is often brutally reminded by Mick of an ordered social world to which he does not belong. Then Mick's remarks about references, solicitors, contracts, personal medical attendants, and so on expose Davies's vulnerability in the face of a world in which he counts for nothing. But Davies's life is filled with other menaces, too. He is frightened that people representing authority might question him about having only four insurance stamps on his card. Even everyday household appliances terrify him.

Davies's response to all this is to be violent himself. Early in

Act One, he promises to revenge himself upon the Scotsman who offended him. On two occasions in the play, he draws a knife, firstly on Mick in Act Two, and then on Aston in Act Three.

Power

Power is seen as primitive, selfish and assertive. It is inseparably bound up with territory (in this case the room) and the struggle for supremacy within that territory. Although the theme is presented primarily through Davies and Mick, even Aston at the end exerts his power and banishes the outsider from what he considers to be his own sphere of influence.

To begin with Davies. In order to secure his position in the room (and therefore his safety from a hostile world outside), Davies attempts to ingratiate himself with Mick once he learns that the apartment is his. By doing so, he hopes to drive a wedge between the two brothers and oust Aston. Having associated himself with someone he sees as powerful, Davies assumes some of the trappings of power. Although Pinter presents these trappings – high expectations of what Aston should be doing for him; the smoking jacket which he associates with the leisured, powerful classes, for example – as pathetic, comic, and illusory, they none the less show that the urge to dominate and influence is a primal one.

With Mick, the case is different. Whereas for Davies power is seen principally in terms of territory and social status, with Mick it offers the sadistic pleasure of dominating and harassing another individual. Mick achieves this partly through physical violence (the end of Act One), but mainly through his abrupt changes of tone and attitude when conversing with Davies. He plays with Davies as an angler plays with a fish, allowing him so much line and then reeling him abruptly in, encouraging confidence and then dashing it. There is an intellectual delight in exercising this kind of domination which is different from the desperate attempts of Davies to find a niche.

There is, too, the power represented by society and its institutions. This comes through in several ways. Society, for instance, can lobotomize Aston and deny him his full humanity; it can terrorize Davies's imagination in the form of figures of authority who might be looking for him because he has only four stamps on his card; and in the form of home owners with the police and the law on their side it can finally eject Davies back onto the streets.

Failure to communicate

In *The Caretaker*, all three characters, but especially Aston and Davies, feel a desperate need to communicate, to express something about themselves to others, but resist doing so in case they expose weaknesses which others might exploit. This tension between our wish to unburden ourselves and our fear of exposing ourselves is a staple Pinter theme. He presents it not only through what the characters say, but through the silences and pauses that punctuate the action. As the action progresses, we come to see these pauses as having a vital dramatic function. For instance, towards the end of Aston's speech which closes Act Two, his pauses suggest a mind recalling things almost too dreadful to put into words. In Davies's final speech, his broken phrases, separated by pauses, communicate very effectively how all communication between him and Aston has now failed. When the pauses occur between speeches they have a variety of functions. For instance, early in Act One, when Davies talks to Aston about sleeping in draughty places, the pauses clearly show that Davies is angling for a bed for the night but feels too awkward to ask outright.

Language in *The Caretaker* is often used to ease the terror characters have of silence rather than to communicate anything. Davies is an interesting example of this. It is quite clear from his appearance that he is a failure and always has been. And so he is driven to create, through language, quite a different impression of himself, not as he is but as he would like to be seen. Language thus becomes a means of hiding the truth about oneself rather than revealing it. His absurd story about why he left his wife is intended to impress Aston by revealing the high standards of propriety he sets himself. And his references to his papers in Sidcup are designed to convince both Aston and Mick that he is man with a secure identity. Pinter seems to be suggesting the double bind in which humanity finds itself. People are frightened of silence but are also frightened of revealing too much about themselves. So they use words to create an impression of who they are, but how they speak and what they speak about inevitably give them away.

Like Davies, Mick also uses language to evade real communication, but he does so in a different way. Davies wants people to have a better impression of himself than he deserves; Mick wants to confuse and frighten them. In his long outbursts in Act Two he clearly intends to bewilder Davies. His varied and incongruous list of details ranging from the Salvation Army, to Red Indians, to Mick's uncle Sid, to a list of London bus routes, to legal and financial jargon not only frightens Davies, but also hides Mick's identity. At the end of the play, despite everything Mick has said, we feel that we know little about him. Whereas Davies fails to hide himself behind the screen of language, Mick is much more successful.

Ironically, though, when characters do feel the need to communicate their deepest feelings, there is no one to listen carefully or sympathetically. This happens to Aston at the end of Act Two when he speaks of his experience in the hospital. As he becomes absorbed in recounting this crucial memory, it becomes clear that Aston is addressing himself rather than anyone else. He – and we – forget about Davies's presence. However, Davies makes cruel use of parts of what he hears later. In expressing his deepest feelings, Aston has merely rendered himself more vulnerable.

Davies and Mick, too, feel an inner compulsion to communicate. In Act Three, Mick describes his ambitions about decorating the flat. A little later, when he laces up the shoes Aston has brought him, Davies moves from his usual complaints about the weather, to ruminating about the hardness of the roads on the way to Sidcup, the way he kept going even though the weather was bad and he nearly died. The speech gives a wonderful insight into the way he keeps his spirits up by praising himself, but shows too how vulnerable he is. But Aston has already departed, and Davies is denied a sympathetic ear.

Loneliness and betrayal

Davies and Aston are both lonely, although for different reasons. Driven in upon himself, trusting no one, Davies sees the world as filled with threat. As such, he functions as a symbol of the isolated nature of the human being. But Pinter makes our response to him more complex than this by heavily qualifying any sympathy we have for Davies. For one thing, he is shown kindness and trust by Aston only to betray him. Too late he realizes that Aston has been a good friend to him. The ease with which Davies betrays Aston indicates why he is lonely: trusting no one himself, he betrays the one man who has shown him trust. But there is more to Davies's loneliness than this. He is not only disloyal, but racist, demanding, quick-tempered and foul-smelling. Davies's loneliness is to a large degree self-induced.

Pinter explores these two themes in a different way through Aston. Like Davies, Aston is lonely; his offer of a bed and a job to Davies suggest this. But whereas Davies's loneliness is at least in part the result of his offensiveness, this is not the case with Aston. If we are to believe Aston's soliloquy at the end of Act Two, his present loneliness is the result of a series of betrayals: firstly by one of the people to whom he used to talk at the factory and the café, secondly by Authority which demands social conformity, and then by his mother who signed the consent form for his operation. His betrayal by Davies is only one further example of how untrustworthy human beings can be.

Davies and Aston, then, are lonely for different reasons: Davies because he is selfish, Aston because he is not. Through them, Pinter shows how people yearn for companionship, but exploit it when they have it, or are exploited when they offer it.

Other Themes

Dreams and aspirations feature significantly in *The Caretaker*. As we have seen, each of the three characters has hopes for the future, none of which is likely to be achieved, but each of which gives some point and purpose to their lives: Davies has his journey to Sidcup; Aston his shed; and Mick his plans to convert the flat into a luxurious apartment. It is through such dreams, Pinter suggests, that we give ourselves identity and provide focus and hope to our lives.

Another way of defining our identity is by what we say of our *past*. But Pinter presents us with an insoluble problem in the play, for there is no way of verifying anything the characters say. Aston might be telling the truth about his operation, or he might *believe* he is telling the truth, or, unlikely but not impossible, he might be lying. We have no way of knowing. Similarly, Davies's stories about himself might be pure fabrication or have a grain of truth. In *The Caretaker*, as in *The Birthday Party*, Pinter explores the hazy line between truth and fiction. We suspect that much of what Davies says about himself is untrue, but he might actually believe what he is saying. We rely upon memories of our past to help define our present identity, but memory can be unreliable, distorting those very incidents it recalls.

Setting and structure

The entire action of the play takes place in one room, which itself contributes to the mood and thematic development. On an obvious level of symbolism, the room, with its clutter of incongruous objects, helps us to understand the clutter of Aston's mind. But there is more to the room than this. For one thing, it allows Pinter to explore an idea which features often in his plays – that is, the disruptive intrusion of an outsider (or outsiders) into an established and safe environment. Although the room belongs to Mick, it is Aston's identity which it most represents. In this room he is safe from the outside world. Davies seeks to oust him and establish himself in his place. Although Davies has to contend with the menacing figure of Mick in the room, it is far more secure than the outside world which is shown to be cold and threatening. Through his use of the room, Pinter shows the primitive need of mankind for warmth and security, and the lengths to which the outsider will go in order to try to secure his share of warmth. In this respect the play has all the power of a parable.

The small number of characters, and the apparent simplicity of the plot, disguise the craft which has gone into the structure of the play. Each act builds to a memorable climax which focuses attention on one of the characters. Act One concludes with the unexpected violence of Mick; Act Two with Aston's disturbing soliloquy; Act Three with the pathetic whining of Davies, whose attempt to secure his place in the room has ironically resulted in his expulsion.

More subtle is the way in which Pinter uses his three characters to impose a dramatic pattern upon the action. Mick's presence is required on stage at the start because it establishes a connection between him and the room and therefore implies a reason for his violent behaviour towards Davies, even if it is a reason the audience does not understand. In Act One, Pinter gives Davies and Aston prominence, allowing Davies especially to establish himself.

In Acts Two and Three, Pinter confirms Davies as the central figure, his developing relationship with Aston and Mick being shown in alternate sequences with one or other of the brothers.

In this way, Pinter shows Mick's dominance over Davies, and Davies's willingness to exploit and betray Aston's kindness.

The play is given unity not only by the careful patterning of the episodes involving Davies and one or other of the brothers, but also by the repetition of key words, phrases and actions. Among the most important of these are Aston's persistent fiddling with the electric plug and his comments about the shed, Davies's need for shoes, his journey to Sidcup, the fact that he smells, his fear of the gas stove, the noises he makes when he is sleeping, and his complaints about the draught. These recurring preoccupations show how little has changed by the end of the play. Davies is once more an outcast, and the odd though powerful relationship between Mick and Aston is as strong as ever.

Language

One of Pinter's greatest gifts as a playwright is his ability to convey the apparent illogicality and repetitions of everyday language. In *The Caretaker*, he uses this to particular effect with Davies. A good example occurs in Act One, leading up to Davies's story about the monastery in Luton. The roundabout way in which Davies tells this story, taking in a friend who runs a public convenience in Shepherd's Bush, another friend in Acton, and a query about the colour of Aston's neighbours, shows brilliantly how his mind works by subjective association rather than clear logic: mention of the monks recalls the friend who told him of them; this recalls another friend (the bootmaker in Acton); this contrasts with his hostility towards his treatment by the monks; which in turn prompts him to voice another deep-rooted hostility – towards the Blacks.

Pinter gives Mick another kind of language. Mick can be a man of few words or crazily inventive in his speech. He can also use language to suggest social superiority. He does this, for example, in his first long speech in Act Two when he refers to his uncle's brother having a *penchant* for nuts.

General questions on *The Caretaker*

1 By selecting your material carefully from each of the three acts, show how Davies becomes increasingly ungrateful for what Aston does for him.

Suggested notes for essay answer:
a) grateful for money, somewhere to stay, but even here grudgingly expressed; b) growing signs of ingratitude over draught; litany of complaints in Act Three about Aston's silence, refusal to move cooker, failure to supply breadknife and clock, habit of waking Davies up. This question requires careful selection of material to show the *developing* nature of Davies's ingratitude. Beginning with the occasional complaint, such as not being able to make a cup of tea, it has become virtually all-consuming by Act Three. Consider the point, too, that Pinter is showing that Davies's demands are insatiable and therefore no matter what is done for him he will always be ungrateful. His complaints against Aston become increasingly ridiculous. He *might* have a point about the draught from the window, but his demands for a breadknife and a clock are merely to gratify his status, not his essential needs. Discuss the fact that Davies's ingratitude is directed against the very person who is kindest to him.

2 Do you have any sympathy for Davies? You might wish to consider the following points: his age; the way people treat him; his need to be respected; the security that the room offers him.

3 Much of *The Caretaker* seems to be unrealistic. What have you found to be realistic about it? You might wish to consider the following points: the way in which the characters speak; the dreams and ambitions they have; their capacity to be cruel, selfish and kind.

4 Write about the difficulties that the characters have in communicating with each other.

5 Look carefully at the episodes in which Davies is offered the job of caretaker first by Aston and then by Mick. In what ways are they different, and what does this suggest to you about Davies?

6 Write an essay showing how different Mick and Aston are. Remember to support your answer by close reference to the play.

7 Imagine that you are Davies. Write the speech he might make the night Aston has told him to leave.

8 By careful reference to the play, show how power is one of the principal ideas presented.

9 'Comedy of menace.' How accurate a description of *The Caretaker* is this?

10 What, if anything, does the play gain by being set in one room?

11 What do you learn about the characters from the dreams, memories and illusions they have?

12 If you were asked to say what you thought were the most distinctive features of *The Caretaker*, how would you answer?

13 Discuss the importance of setting in any other book you have read.

14 Show how the idea of betrayal is presented in any other book you have read.

15 Discuss the presentation of an outcast or a misfit in a book of your choice.

The Homecoming

Act Commentaries with textual notes and revision questions

Act One

Pages 7–19

From the outset, the themes of menace, selfishness and verbal abuse are apparent. Max persists in asking his son, Lenny, about the newspaper he is looking for, while Lenny's reply shows a complete lack of respect. When Max finally gives up looking for the paper, sits down and lights a cigarette, his reminiscences are important because they introduce two figures who, though they never appear in the play, cast a large shadow over it: MacGregor (Max's friend) and Max's wife, Jessie. His remark that Mac was fond of Jessie might seem innocent enough, but in Pinter little is ever mentioned that is not of dramatic importance and our curiosity is aroused about the nature of their relationship. (Sam's comments about Jessie a little later in this section also make us wonder what kind of woman she was.) Max gives no reason for hating her so much and we are left wondering why Mac was so fond of her. We sense here, and throughout the play, that the characters know (or suspect) more than we do, and we follow events hoping for clarification. Max's comments bring another brusque response from Lenny, who, almost in the same breath, asks his father's opinion about a horse race. This mixture of insult and dependence is a feature of the relationship of the whole family (Teddy excluded) that Pinter explores in the play. Lenny's enquiry prompts a dismissive reply from Max, who launches into another reminiscence, this time about his knowledge of horse racing. How true these memories are cannot be verified, but the purpose of this one is clear enough: to belittle his son by boasting of his own accomplishments. Lenny insults him again, and when threatened pleads mockingly in the voice of a child not to be beaten.

When Sam, Max's brother, enters in his chauffeur's uniform, he provides another target for the mockery and malice of Lenny and Max. Lenny's tone is teasing as he asks about Sam's day. Max is more openly hostile, helping himself to one of Sam's cigars before he is offered it and then persistently questioning his brother about a remark made by the American Sam had driven to the airport. Max's hostility increases as he questions Sam about why he never married. Sam is clearly offended, but is reluctant to be aggressive in return. When he speaks of Jessie, he does so tenderly, and is anxious to assure his brother that although he took Jessie out once or twice in the car, he was always aware that she was his brother's wife. This remark makes us wonder if Jessie was the source of friction between the two brothers, which would account for Max's behaviour to Sam.

Joey, Lenny's younger brother, returns from the gymnasium where he has been training to become a boxer. After Lenny has departed, Max wastes little time in giving Joey advice, and in a fine comic speech indicates that Joey's only weaknesses as a boxer are that he cannot attack, and he cannot defend himself! Joey leaves and Max and Sam are alone. Insults and threats soon fly. Sam persists in trying to convince Max that nothing untoward happened between himself and Jessie in the car, making us increasingly curious about what actually did occur. A new side to Sam's character is revealed when, from being passive and emollient, he adopts Max's foulmouthed, sarcastic tone. He begins by abusing MacGregor, and then remarks casually that MacGregor, of course, was a good friend of Max, thereby implying that Max has poor taste in friends. This section closes with Max's speech about his father. It is an excellent example of Pinter's use of ambiguity; the speech is at once wistful and bitter.

Many times I was offered the job ... needed me at home. Max's failure to remember the name of the Duke might be genuine, but it might also indicate that the whole speech is a fabrication, designed to increase his self-esteem and impress Lenny.

I don't press myself on people ... the time of day when required. Note the pride Sam takes in the job he does and the car he drives. Such pride makes him a target for Max's scathing sarcasm.

Humber Super Snipe A luxurious car, popular in the 1960s.

Flying Fortress A large American cargo plane.

What have you been doing, banging away at your lady customers ... Other people Banging away is slang for having sexual intercourse. This is an important sequence. It not only shows Max's vulgarity but leaves us wondering if Sam's final remark might actually apply to someone in particular – Jessie, for instance.

Dorchester An expensive London hotel.

I want to make something clear about Jessie ... I want to remind you. There does seem to be something obsessive about Sam's wish to convince Max that *he* never took advantage of Jessie. Also, his remark that Max would not have trusted Mac is interesting, considering, that Mac was Max's friend.

Pages 19–24

With the entrance of Teddy and Ruth, Pinter has introduced all his characters. Teddy's pleasure at being home is evident in the way he smiles, but what is equally important is the way he behaves toward Ruth and she toward him. Although he is attentive to her, he soon becomes hesitant, as if he is uncertain of what to say to her. Ruth for her part seems curiously muted. This could, of course, be tiredness or even nervousness, but her asking Teddy if he wants to stay is odd considering that they have only just arrived. Teddy's concern for Ruth continues when he suggests that she goes to bed. We notice that Teddy is doing most of the talking, but his tone is strained. Ruth, although she says comparatively little, is shown to have a mind of her own. She declines Teddy's suggestions quietly but firmly, making us wonder exactly where the power lies in this relationship. On two occasions in this section, Ruth makes remarks that suggest that her passivity is not the same as docility: firstly, there is a hint of mockery when she comments to Teddy that his room can't have moved; secondly, her assertion that she isn't making any noise shows a willingness to stand up for herself. Her determination, as well as her ability to shake Teddy's confidence, is further demonstrated when she says she is going for a stroll. Teddy's attempt to impose his will upon her fails, and when he asks her what he is going to do if she goes for a stroll, we see his dependence on her.

This section is an excellent example of the economy of Pinter's writing. Within a few pages we have to revise fundamentally our opinion of the marriage of Ruth and Teddy. At the start everything that happens has a perfectly natural explanation: Teddy's behaviour could spring from his nervousness at bringing his wife home for the first time, Ruth could simply be tired or worried about meeting her in-laws. Yet as the section continues we realize that these explanations are unsatisfactory and superficial. It is much more likely that Pinter is hinting at underlying tensions in their marriage which later events will bring to the surface.

She looks at him. Pinter suggests a great deal here. Teddy has asked
Ruth a question to which she does not reply: she simply looks at him.
There are any number of explanations, but the most likely one is that
she has no wish to speak to him. His fear of silence between them
prompts him to start speaking again. Silence does not daunt her.

What do you think of the room? ... My mother was dead. Another
fine example of Teddy's need to talk, although the difficulty he finds
in speaking to his wife is further evidence of the distance between
them. Also evident here is Teddy's sad need to boast about the room.

I think ... the children ... might be missing us. Ironic words in the
light of what Ruth does in the final act.

suddenly chews his knuckles. A small, but important, sign of Teddy's
nervousness.

Pages 25–27

Teddy's meeting with a brother he has not seen for years could
hardly be less enthusiastic. Having just described them to Ruth
as very warm people, we see, in fact, that Lenny and Teddy have
nothing to say to each other apart from a few banal pleasantries
of the kind strangers make. Their awkwardness is highlighted
by the many pauses in their conversation.

Pages 27–35

By contrast, Lenny has a great deal to say to Ruth, a woman he
has never met before. To begin with, it is Lenny who appears to
be the more assured, casually introducing himself, mockingly
offering Ruth an aperitif (an inappropriate drink for that time
of day; see note below) and then admitting that in fact there is
not a drink in the house. His apparent ignorance that Ruth is
Teddy's wife comes as a surprise, and suggests that Teddy has
not visited his family for many years and has had no communication with them. In Act Two, however, Sam mentions that
Teddy has written to Max, which makes Lenny's attitude here all
the more curious. It is possible, of course, that Max has not
bothered to tell him that Teddy has married Ruth. It is equally
possible that Lenny knows precisely who Ruth is, but feigns
ignorance because he hopes to embarrass her and therefore
establish his predominance over this stranger in the house.

From very early in this section, there is a subtle menace about
Lenny's behaviour toward Ruth. He makes no direct response to

being told that she is Teddy's wife, but instead launches on a long speech about the clock ticking. Although he begins by asking for Ruth's advice about the clock (an odd request to make to a total stranger), he is in fact not interested in anything she might have to say, but instead dominates the occasion by talking himself. His remark that he bets she could do with a glass of water is designed, by its very absurdity, to make her feel uncomfortable. Later comments, such as his father being chuffed to his bollocks (vulgarity), and Teddy and Ruth visiting Italy before visiting their family (accusing), have the same effect.

Lenny's aggressive attitude continues with his nonsensical remarks about Venice, and then become more openly violent in his speech about the prostitute at the docks and the old lady and the mangle. Instead of feeling threatened by all this, as she is clearly meant to do, Ruth remains poised, refusing to give him her glass of water, calling him Leonard (which he dislikes) and then thoroughly shocking him (and us) by offering herself to him. This section has revealed a complete reversal in the relationship between the two, with Ruth moving to a position of dominance. The power she exerts so effortlessly over the two men with whom she has appeared so far fixes her at the heart of the play.

aperitif An alcoholic drink taken before lunch or dinner to stimulate the appetite. Lenny's use of the word here is ambiguous. Either he is trying to impress Ruth but unintentionally uses an inappropriate word to comic effect; or he deliberately uses the word knowing that she will realize he is mocking her. Given Lenny's command of language elsewhere, the second possibility seems more likely.

One night . . . sort of left it at that Lenny's speech raises many issues. It might be a pack of lies designed to discomfort Ruth. It might be true, in which case it shows that Lenny's capacity for violence is not only verbal. And the mention of the chauffeur makes us wonder if Sam was in any way involved in the incident.

all quiet on the Western Front The Western Front was an area of conflict in World War I; *All Quiet on the Western Front* is the title of a novel by Erich Maria Remarque about the war. Lenny's reference to the novel shows that the calm of the docks is illusory, a point which is made clear by what happens to the woman almost immediately after.

He's always been my favourite brother . . . as sensitive as he is. Besides the obvious mockery of Teddy for being sensitive, Lenny is also mocking Ruth by telling her something about himself which is so obviously untrue. As the relish with which he tells his two violent stories shows, he has no wish to be sensitive.

That's the name my mother gave me. Note the ambiguity Pinter
creates in this statement. It could hint at Lenny's dislike of his mother
(possibly because, as Sam says later, Teddy was her favourite) and
therefore his contempt for women in general; or it could show such a
deep devotion to her that he does not want a strange woman like Ruth
using the name his beloved mother used.

Pages 35–37

This little sequence between Max and Lenny offers a neat contrast with the previous scene, in that together they show two
different ways of dealing with Lenny. Aroused by Lenny's
shouting, Max comes downstairs to find out what is going on.
Lenny does not mention Ruth, but instead makes enquiries of
his father about his own conception. His questions are clearly
designed to be offensive and they have the effect of making Max
so angry that he spits at his son. This contrasts markedly with the
cool but effective way in which Ruth dealt with Lenny, and
shows that in this house of men, a woman can achieve consider-
able power.

Look . . . pop off, eh? An insult meaning why don't you drop dead?
since you're in the mood for a bit of a . . . chat Notice how the slight
pause before the word *chat* allows Lenny to emphasize the sarcasm in
his voice.

Pages 37–44

This section begins with Joey doing some limbering-up exercises. From the way he stops to comb his hair carefully, and then
watches himself in the mirror as he shadow-boxes, we become
more aware of his vanity. Max resents Sam being in the kitchen
washing up the dishes. When Sam appears, Max takes the
opportunity to argue with him and belittle him. Into this
unpleasant atmosphere come Teddy and Ruth. Instead of
greeting his son, Max takes it as a personal insult that he was not
informed of his arrival, and then becomes abusive to Ruth. Even
when Teddy tells his father that he and Ruth are married, Max
persists in his gross insults, finally telling Joey to throw them out
of the house. Pinter offers no easy explanation for Max's
behaviour; Joey's comment that Max is an old man is not entirely

satisfactory. We sense there are deeper reasons for Max's anger – possibly as father, and therefore head of the house, he feels threatened by the return of his eldest son; perhaps he feels ashamed because of something that happened between himself and Teddy in the past; he might even feel that other members of his family are 'ganging-up' against him by not telling him of his son's arrival home. His treatment of Ruth might be connected with his dislike of women, especially when we remember the references earlier on to his wife. What is important, though, is not which of these is 'right', but what effect his behaviour has. For one thing, it sustains the atmosphere of violence and abuse which is central to the whole play; for another, it hints that there is a whole layer of secret guilt and fear festering beneath the surface, corroding the relationships between the relations.

The violence breaks out physically when Max punches Joey and hits Sam with his stick. Then, as though he is emotionally exhausted, Max changes his behaviour toward Teddy and warmly welcomes him home.

Revision questions and assignments on Act One

1 Examine carefully the scene between Ruth and Lenny and show how Pinter manages to create a sense of threat.

2 Referring closely to Act One, show how Max and Sam have different personalities.

3 What evidence is there in Act One that Ruth is stronger and more determined than Teddy?

4 Write a brief character study of Joey.

5 In what ways is the past important in Act One?

Act Two

Pages 45–53

Act Two opens on what appears to be a united family. Ruth hands coffee to the men, Max smiles at her, she compliments him on a fine lunch and he expresses pleasure that she liked it. In this seemingly relaxed mood, he begins to reminisce about his wife, praising her qualities as a mother and musing about the pride she would have felt in her grandchildren (who, in any case, are in America). The idealized picture he creates of her contrasts with what he said of her to Sam early in Act One. His fantasy continues as he creates an idyllic portrait of his early married life in a closely-knit family – a loving, hard-working father, a kind mother and shiny-faced children. The evidence of the play does not support this. It is Ruth who breaks this sentimental mood by asking him what happened to the group of butchers he joined, to which Max bluntly replies that they were a bunch of criminals. What is important here is that it is Ruth – a woman – who, by asking the question, challenges Max's daydreams. One begins to wonder to what extent the other woman in the play (Jessie) did the same thing; moments after speaking so nostalgically of his wife and family he launches into a fierce criticism of them, and then of Sam. This unpredictability in Max, rather than making him less credible, makes him more so. He is an embittered old man, by turns venomous and sentimental.

After Sam has left for work, Max talks warmly to Teddy, telling him how pleased he is to have his eldest son home. His regret that Teddy and Ruth decided to marry secretly develops into a wish that Lenny and Joey would marry too. He adopts here the role of loving parent, anxious for the happiness of his children, seeking reconciliation with his eldest son, and proud of his achievements. Yet whenever he speaks in this manner, we remember the viciousness of his tongue and the divisiveness of his manner.

For the first part of the conversation between Teddy and Max, Ruth is silent, but when she does speak, she again arouses our curiosity. Her first words – that she is sure Teddy is happy because Max approves of her – show her to be clever at ingratiating herself. From the cool, poised way she dealt with Lenny earlier, we sense that she is very much her own woman; yet here she presents herself as the docile, conventional wife, anxious for her father-in-law's approval. Her hesitant remarks about being different when she first met Teddy suggest a troubled conscience and a dark secret, but Pinter does nothing to satisfy our curiosity at this stage by explaining more clearly what she means. He thus generates dramatic suspense.

As Teddy speaks warmly of his success as a professor and his good fortune in having such a wonderful wife (we note the echoes of Max's remarks about Jessie at the start of the act and wonder whether to believe Teddy's account), Lenny joins the conversation. He questions Teddy about some philosophical ideas which he says interest him. Effortlessly, Lenny bursts the bubble of Teddy's academic confidence, pushing him onto the defensive and revealing him to be the hesitant character of whom we had a glimpse when he first appeared with Ruth. Naturally, this makes us wonder if he is as successful as he would like his family to think.

What is equally important, though, is the way in which Ruth deals with Lenny. Whereas Teddy is unable to respond with any force to Lenny's question about the philosophical idea of the certainty of existence, Ruth does so by drawing Lenny's attention to the existence of her body which, she claims, clearly exists. This blatant piece of sexual provocation (the second time she has spoken to Lenny in this way) makes us wonder again quite what it was that she did before she met Teddy. After this there is an awkward silence, before she drifts into a reverie about her six years in America. From her references to the rock, sand and insects, we gather that she does not like it. The idyllic picture that Teddy had painted moments earlier has been smashed.

I was busy working twenty-four hours a day in the shop. This does not sit happily with Max's claim in Act One to be an expert on horse-racing.

a dress of pale corded . . . lilac flowered taffeta. The delicate detail Max uses here is at odds with his usual foul manner of speaking, and hints that it is fantasy.

I remember the boys came down . . . Jessie's and mine This picture of the happy family is so stereotyped and sentimental as to be clearly untrue.

You'd bend over for half a dollar on Blackfriars Bridge. Max insults Sam by suggesting he's a homosexual prostitute.

my two youngsters This is an odd way of describing Lenny and Joey. Max is once more assuming the role of loving father.

Doctor of Philosophy The highest academic degree that can be awarded to a student.

Who cares? . . . live in the past? Max's advice to Teddy to live in the present is something which, ironically, he is unable to do himself.

She's a great help . . . environment. Notice how the pauses in Teddy's speech suggest that he is not entirely convinced by what he is saying.

Do you detect . . . Christian theism? 'Do you think that the Christian idea of God is illogical?' Notice that Lenny's tone and vocabulary become much more formal and 'academic' here. He is clearly ridiculing Teddy.

I've got a couple of friends . . . always saying things like that. The idea of Lenny discussing philosophical issues in the bar of an hotel is highly improbable. His ridicule of Teddy is more blatant here.

TEDDY *stands.* Teddy is disturbed by the suggestive manner in which Ruth speaks.

Pages 53-55

This important little section shows how much on the defensive Teddy now is. His return home as the successful eldest son who will impress his family with his academic achievements and desirable style of life has instead seen his intellectual humiliation by a younger brother, and his wife's flaunting herself before that same brother. There is also evidence of Ruth's unhappiness in America (her words at the close of the previous section). As a result, Teddy is anxious to leave. We notice how he tries to persuade Ruth that they should go by mentioning their boys, their lovely home, and the help she can give him with his lectures. Ruth, however, shows no such eagerness. Instead, she remains noncommittal, again showing that of the two she is the more powerful. Toward the end of the section, Teddy is reduced to feeble boasting about being able to speak Italian. It is as though he already senses that he is losing Ruth. Desperate to leave, he goes upstairs to pack their suitcases. What was meant to have been a triumphant return home is turning into a nightmare.

fall semester The half-yearly period in an American university beginning in the autumn.

Italian campaign i.e. in World War II. Notice how Ruth rejects Teddy's boast that he brought her happiness by taking her to Italy by suggesting that had she been been a nurse during the war she would have gone anyway.

Pages 56-62

Events move rapidly in this important section of the play. Lenny enters and he and Ruth make polite, but banal, conversation for a while about winter coming, and then about clothes. Ruth announces that she was a model before she went to America.

Lenny assumes the obvious meaning of the word and asks if she modelled hats and recounts briefly an occasion when he bought a girl a hat. Ruth corrects him by stating that she was a photographic model; that is, she posed naked or semi-naked for magazines. At the time the play was written, this was considered disreputable employment, little better than, and often related to, prostitution. This is clearly what she meant earlier when she said she had been different before she married Teddy. Almost as if the burden of confession is too great for her, she drifts into an incoherent recollection of going to a large house in the country to do her modelling. Pinter does not make it clear why this memory should stay with her, but although it is vague, we sense, too, that it is important to her. It is possible that she remembers that period of her life as a time of comparative freedom compared with the boredom and orthodoxy of marriage to Teddy.

Teddy enters with the suitcases and demands to know what Lenny has been saying to her, but his attempt to impose himself upon the scene is entirely ineffective. Lenny puts on some music and asks Ruth to dance with him. As they dance, he kisses her. All Teddy can do is stand helplessly holding her coat. Max and Joey watch them dance and kiss. Delighted that Lenny has a 'tart', Joey takes Ruth from his brother and treats her in a sexually belittling way. We notice that as far as Joey is concerned, she is no longer Ruth, his sister-in-law, but a tart, someone he can sexually exploit. Ruth at this point appears submissive and compliant, a passive object to be used by men. What follows is a brilliant piece of grotesque comedy. While Ruth is being sexually fondled by both Lenny and Joey, Max makes small-talk about what a beautiful wife Teddy has, and what a wonderful mother she must be. As his language becomes more ironical, and therefore less applicable to Ruth, we realize that he is not only mocking Teddy for being so weak, but Ruth, too, for being so sluttish. It is as though she confirms his worst impressions of women.

The image of Ruth being dominated by men quickly changes. Having used her body to entice men to her, she now exerts her power over them. She pushes Joey away, stands up and demands something to drink and something to eat. She is peremptory and scathing, criticizing the glass in which Lenny brings the whisky, and mocking his use of the American term 'on the rocks'. We note how quickly Lenny and Joey comply with her wishes. She has now become a powerful woman in the house, having humiliated her husband and shown a capacity to dominate his brothers. As this goes on, Teddy vainly tries to regain some dignity by speaking of the importance of his work and claiming it is too difficult for his family to understand. But his attempt to show his superiority fails pathetically, and in the closing speech of this section he is reduced to virtual incoherence, destroyed by the physical desire of his brothers and by the determined bid for power within the family made by his wife.

Well, the evenings are drawing in . . . Just before we went to America Notice in this long section how Pinter uses pauses for dramatic effect. For instance, the pauses early on show the awkwardness of two people finding it difficult to carry on a conversation. Then Ruth's pause before she says that she used to be a model hints that her remark is going to be important and provocative. Later pauses, as she makes her long speech, suggest the difficulty she has in speaking of those occasions when she went to the house in the country.

cloche The veiling was bell-shaped.

Look, next time you come over . . . you're married or not The mockery is cruel here because of the offhand way in which Max suggests that Teddy has lost his wife.

I'm broadminded An understatement considering what is taking place in the room.

on the rocks? With ice? Lenny's use of this American expression brings a sarcastic response from Ruth.

We've got rocks . . . But they're frozen stiff in the fridge A weak explanation which shows how much Ruth dominates Lenny at this moment.

LENNY **_hands drinks all round_** This, together with his enquiry a moment later if Ted wants soda, adds to the bitter comedy of the scene. Lenny behaves as though nothing unusual has happened.

Pages 62–65

It is evening. Teddy, still in his coat, is alone with Sam who asks him his opinion of MacGregor. That Sam should ask such questions of Teddy shows how largely MacGregor features in Sam's mind, making us wonder what the reason can be. His gratitude to Teddy for writing to him shows how sad a figure he really is. Interestingly, he says that Teddy was his mother's favourite son, a possible reason why the other members of his family dislike him.

Lenny enters and asks if anyone has seen his cheese roll. When Teddy answers that he has taken it, Sam, sensing trouble, leaves the room. Teddy's confession that he took the roll deliberately shows how pathetic a figure he has become. Unable to counter his humiliation in any effective way, all he can do is steal and eat his brother's cheese roll. However, this is not the end of the matter. Beginning with a sense of personal shock that Teddy could have done something so mean-spirited as to steal his roll, Lenny develops the idea that Teddy has somehow let the whole family down by his lack of generosity. The entire speech is rich in irony. Lenny is outraged at having lost a cheese sandwich and speaks animatedly about it; Teddy is merely abject at having lost his wife. Pinter has turned received values on their head. Lenny demands an apology from Teddy for taking his cheese roll, seemingly quite unaware that what he has done to his elder brother is far less pardonable. By pushing his ridiculous claims to the limit, Lenny appears to be daring Teddy to disagree with him, to become furious at the way he has been treated. But Teddy does not respond. All he does is give a monosyllabic answer to Lenny's final questions.

Still here, Ted? . . . seminar Lenny's casual remark is, of course, sarcastic, as is his use of the word 'seminar' – a meeting of a group of university students with a lecturer at which one of them presents a paper on a given topic which is then discussed.

Mind you . . . more forthcoming, not less. Notice how Lenny's repetition of 'old' and 'and all that' show how he is sneering at Teddy's way of life.

Greyhound buses Buses that cover the length and breadth of the USA enabling people to travel vast distances quite cheaply.

I'm busy with my occupation At this stage we do not know what it is.

je ne sais quoi Again Lenny is mocking Teddy by using this French term, which means literally 'I don't know what'.

Pages 65–74

The mood of the play becomes more grotesque when we realize that while this conversation has been taking place between Lenny and Teddy, Joey has been upstairs in bed with Ruth. When Joey enters, his remarks to Lenny are not quite precise enough for us to be sure what he means. But it soon becomes clear. When he announces that they did not actually have sexual intercourse, Lenny is incredulous. He is convinced that Ruth is a tease and asks Teddy for confirmation. The comedy of the interchange is the bleakest imaginable, as they speak to each other of Teddy's wife in front of him as if she were a common prostitute, which in a sense she now is, while referring to her as Teddy's wife when they speak to him.

Teddy's sour remark that perhaps Joey failed with Ruth because he lacked the right touch, brings Lenny quickly to his younger brother's defence at the expense of the elder. Girls, he claims, find Joey irresistible, and he proceeds to describe, with Joey's help, an unpleasant incident which is meant to demonstrate Joey's charm. Late one night, the two brothers were cruising in their car looking for girls. On finding a parked car with two men and two women in it, Joey told the men to go away. The pauses, together with Joey's coy use of the word 'escorts', implies that there was the threat of violence if the two men did not do as they were told. The menacing nature of the brothers' behaviour is also hinted at by Joey's remark that they got the girls out of the car, the implication being that they did not go willingly. Lenny and Joey drove the girls to some waste ground to have sex with them. Lenny describes the moment when Joey's girl refused to have sex without a contraceptive, citing Joey's reply as an instance of his sense of humour when, in fact, the underlying tone is one of threat. Clearly, Joey forced the girl into having sex with him. The incident itself, together with Lenny's account of it as though it were a funny story, shows the callousness of both brothers and, much more disturbingly, their sadism.

When Max enters and is told that Ruth has not given herself to Joey, he is outraged that she could treat his youngest son so unkindly. The irony here is grotesque, as Max's concern for Joey comes at the expense of his concern for Teddy. With no regard for Teddy's feelings Max asks him bluntly if Ruth behaves that way with him. Drained of any self-respect Teddy actually replies in the negative to this insulting question. Joey becomes angry at Teddy's suggestion that Ruth has sex with Teddy but not with him, taking it as a personal affront. Sam's attempt to give a possible explanation – that Ruth is after all Teddy's wife – is brushed aside.

The conversation moves in a new direction when Max suggests that they keep Ruth with them. Teddy's objection that they have to return to the children is dismissed, as is Sam's that Max is talking rubbish. Taken with the idea, Max, Joey and Lenny quickly work on a plan to keep Ruth for their own use. The materialistic way in which they discuss how to provide for her shows that they regard her merely as a possession. When Lenny remarks that she will be expensive to keep, there is rich irony in Max's reply that there are human considerations besides economic ones. The human considerations he is talking about are their sexual needs, and have nothing to do with human values which are conspicuously absent.

Lenny then makes a new, more attractive, suggestion which extends the cruel, topsy-turvy logic of the scene. Instead of their spending money to keep her, if she became a prostitute she could keep herself, and have time to satisfy their sexual needs as well. The zest with which Max, who is seventy, discusses the idea contributes greatly to the shock effect of the scene. Only Lenny seems to have doubts about the wisdom of the idea, and these doubts are based upon the expense of setting Ruth up rather than the morality of what they are doing; the feelings of Ruth and Teddy are not even considered. Then, by another rich irony, Joey protests that he does not want to share her. The irony here works in several ways. For one thing, he obviously fails to realize that Teddy does not want to share her either. For another, Max's outrage at Joey's arrogance is ironic because he clearly thinks it preferable that his daughter-in-law should become a prostitute and be common to all than that she should remain with only one brother, even if that brother is not her husband. The debased way he regards Ruth is apparent a little later when he reprimands Joey for his selfishness and tells him that if he is not willing to share her, she will be sent back to America. His tone is reminiscent of a father reprimanding a naughty child. (Incidentally, we learn here what Lenny does for a living; he runs a string of prostitutes.)

Teddy's humiliation continues when his father asks him if Ruth is likely to prove a tease (and therefore both a disappointment to them personally and a business failure as a prostitute). His degradation is further compounded when Lenny suggests that he could mention Ruth's name to parties of Americans who are visiting London. He even offers Teddy commission.

Thoroughly worn down, all Teddy can do is suggest that if they keep her so busy she'll get old before her time. But Max, triumphant in the humiliation of his eldest son, caps this by saying that the health service will look after her. At this moment, Ruth, the subject of their conversation, enters.

Alfa Alfa Romeo motor car.

geezers Slang for 'men'.

and then we ... Yes, plenty of rubble. Note how much menace Pinter manages to suggest in this sequence. Joey is not very articulate, but the nasty nature of what happened comes through ordinary words like 'told', 'to go away', and 'got', and his repetition of the word rubble.

the whole hog i.e. the whole way (sexually). By having Lenny and Joey repeat this phrase, Pinter shows how debased their attitude toward women – and sex – is.

the gravy Just as gravy can be the finishing touch to a meal, so Lenny suggests that the finishing touch to Teddy's relationship with Ruth is that she lets him have sex with her. Pinter uses this phrase to the same effect as the one above.

After all, she's not someone off the street, she's my daughter-in-law! The cruel comedy of this line lies in the fact that they are, of course, treating her as though she *is* someone off the streets. The exclamation mark suggests that Max is aware of his joke.

Greek Street A resort of prostitutes in Soho, London.

Savoy An expensive London hotel.

Pan-American An American airline.

Pages 75–82

Although Ruth says very little at the outset, what she does say reveals her total composure. Teddy, in as bland a way as he can manage, tells her that she has been invited to stay a little longer with the family. When Max joins in, he discusses the invitation as though a warm, close-knit family were anxious to retain the company of a much-loved daughter-in-law. Teddy continues in the same evasive way to inform Ruth that because the family is poor, she will be expected to contribute financially. However, Lenny's offer of a flat introduces the business note to the proceedings. We realize with a shock that Ruth, instead of being an innocent victim of three lascivious men, is, in fact, entirely in control of the situation. Although no mention has been made of what she will be expected to do, she immediately understands, making Teddy's polite generalizations seem totally wasted. In the discussion of terms that follows, she proves to be an effective bargainer. When Max, Lenny and Joey discussed the proposition earlier, they saw Ruth as the passive, compliant figure in their plans. Now she dominates them. Briskly, she announces the kind of flat she wants, the conveniences – including a personal maid – she expects, her wardrobe and the drawing up of a contract. In each case, the men give way to her.

Lenny and Max tell her that she will be expected to help around the house, too, and even Teddy, by now actively contributing to his own disgrace, tells her that she will be expected to keep everyone company. At this moment, Sam, who has been silent for some time, comes forward to unburden himself of his great secret: that MacGregor and Jessie had sex in the back of his car as he drove them along. Having stated this he collapses, but is not, to Max's disappointment, dead. Max refuses to believe what Sam has said.

Teddy takes his leave, with Max giving him fatherly advice about the best way to get the airport, the normality of the language contrasting markedly with the extraordinary nature of the situation. Ruth asks him not to become a stranger. With Teddy gone and Sam still unconscious, Ruth assumes her dominant position in the family. As she sits with Joey's head in her lap, Max, jealous that Joey is going to be her favourite, becomes suspicious of her, and suspects that she is going to divide and rule them. Protesting to her that he is not an old man, he has some kind of fit, and falls slowly beside her chair and asks her to kiss him. She continues to stroke Joey's hair.

you're kin. You're kith. You're part of the family. Highly ironic.

You would have to regard your original outlay simply as a capital investment. Ruth drives a hard bargain. She refuses to agree to a loan, which she would have to repay. Instead she says that money Lenny spends on her (his capital outlay) must be regarded as a business investment on his part, and therefore is not repayable.

All aspects of the agreement . . . finalized the contract. The agreement would have to be acceptable to both sides before it was signed.

MacGregor . . . as I drove them along One possible reason for Sam's confession here is that the sight of another woman betraying her husband prompts him to tell everyone about Jessie. Another possibility is that Sam (who is basically decent) is so outraged by Max's part in what has been going on that he wants to humiliate and hurt him in the way that Teddy has been hurt and humiliated.

Revision questions and assignments on Act Two

1 Show how Teddy's degradation becomes more extreme in this act.

2 Choose two incidents which you find comic, and explain what you find comic about them.

3 Using information only from this act, write a character study of Ruth.

4 Joey's character is presented in more detail than it is in Act One. What do you learn about him in this act?

Pinter's art in *The Homecoming*
Characters

Ruth

'I was a model for the body'

An attractive woman in her early thirties, Ruth was born near the house where the action of the play takes place, and so the homecoming is hers, too. Unlike Teddy, she proves to be a resourceful, calculating person, quite willing to exploit her sexuality in order to achieve a position of dominance. She is a figure who is adept at allowing men to think she is vulnerable and then overpowering them when they least expect it.

When we first see her, she seems curiously muted, speaking very little and then mostly in response to what Teddy says. When she asks Teddy if he wants to stay, and suggests the children might be missing her, it is easy to see her as nothing more than a timid wife/mother figure. However, even at this early stage, there are indications that this is not a completely adequate description of her. She is quietly but firmly determined not to go to bed, and equally determined to have a breath of fresh air. We soon begin to suspect that for all Teddy's attempts to present himself as the dominant male, he is the weaker of the two.

This opening sequence with Teddy presents in its mildest form the method of dealing with men which she uses throughout the play, seemingly submissive and vulnerable yet finally proving to be stronger than any of them. It is a feature of her character that is shown more dramatically in her conversation with Lenny. At first the initiative seems to be entirely with him as he mocks and threatens her. She scarcely speaks, but when she does it is to devastating effect. When he finishes the story about the prostitute, for instance, instead of being horrified by his talk of murder, she merely asks how he knew she was diseased. This totally deflates Lenny, who lamely asserts that he decided she was, and then he changes the subject. A little later she makes overtly sexual advances to him. Surprised by having a woman take the initiative so suddenly, Lenny blusters, causing her to laugh at him.

Part of her strength lies in her refusal to be insulted. When

Max first meets her, for instance, he calls her several coarse names; he even asks Teddy if their three children are all his, implying that Ruth might have been unfaithful. Yet throughout all this she never protests, but remains silent, biding her time.

She starts Act Two having been accepted by the family – and therefore able more effectively to compete with them for power. Astutely, she hands coffee to all the men and compliments Max on the lunch he prepared (contrast the way Lenny speaks of Max's cooking in Act One). But despite all this appearance of docility, she can unerringly puncture the pretensions of men. As Max launches into a sentimental story about his wife and children, she bides her time and then asks him about the confederation of butchers he mentioned earlier in the story. His bitter reply – that they were a bunch of crooks – effectively shatters the cosy illusion of a perfect marriage he has been creating.

Yet although she is astute and able to subdue men, she is also vulnerable on occasions. Her remark early in Act Two that she was different when she met Teddy is dismissed by Max, but it indicates a need on her part to confess the truth about herself. She actually confesses to Lenny a little later that she was a photographic model, before she drifts into a half-coherent account of visiting a house in the country a couple of times to do her modelling. Whether it is a happy or a sad memory is hard to tell. What is clear is that Ruth is at present desperately unhappy with her life. The way she speaks so simply yet so movingly of the rock, sand and insects in America illustrates this. Her quiet desperation might explain her behaviour in the latter part of the play. Used by men all her life (by photographers who sold pictures of her; and by Teddy who took her to America), she sees this as her one opportunity to do something for herself and on her own terms. The men in the play consistently underrate her. Believing her to be compliant and docile (her behaviour with Joey on the sofa, for instance), they are surprised by her demanding food and drink. Later, she uses exactly the same tactic. Max, Lenny and Joey discuss putting her on the streets as though she is someone to be manipulated. When she hears of it she is not outraged but demands the best deal for herself. By using her sexuality – her most potent weapon – she establishes authority over the men. Lenny is the only one at the end about whom there is some uncertainty.

Yet Ruth is not an evil woman. Notice that she asks Teddy not to become a stranger. He will, of course, but Ruth does not set out to cause pain; she responds to the world as she finds it; a world in which men will exploit women one way or another – unless the woman is prepared to fight back.

Teddy

'That question doesn't fall within my province'

Teddy, the eldest brother, is a professor of philosophy in America, and as such is the most obviously successful member of the family. It is his return home which precipitates the entire action of the play. Although he tries to pass himself off as a great success, Teddy's weaknesses are apparent from the start. In his opening scene with Ruth, he begins with a reasonable degree of confidence, but it soon becomes apparent that Ruth is more strong-minded than he is. He is attentive to her, telling her not to be nervous, but in fact he is more nervous than she is.

What is meant to be a triumphant homecoming of the success-ful eldest brother gets off to a bad start when he meets Lenny. Clearly he and Lenny have nothing to say to each other. Matters become even worse in the morning when Teddy presents him-self to his father. Instead of welcoming him, Max is abrupt, abusive and suspicious. Teddy clearly no longer fits into the family, if he ever did. We begin to see behind the action of the play an archetypal situation being presented; the return home of the eldest son who presents a threat to the established order within the family. It might be a primitive fear of this kind which unites Max, Joey and Lenny against him. It might even be envy that Teddy was, as Sam says, his mother's favourite. Pinter does not offer any precise explanation of the family's hostility toward Teddy, but even though they might quarrel amongst themselves they invariably unite against him.

In Act Two Teddy's complete humiliation occurs, as the weak-ness in his personality is exposed cruelly by those people amongst whom he should feel safest. First, he is made to look ineffective in a philosophical discussion with Lenny. In response to the precise questions he is asked, all he can do is make excuses. It would seem that he has become so specialized in his subject that he cannot answer any general enquiry at all. Rather than give him any insight into the world, all his studying has done is make him incapable of understanding it.

Secondly, he is made to look indecisive and weak over Ruth. Whereas his intellectual disgrace takes place quickly, this is prolonged over several pages. He is not only a witness to Joey's blatantly sexual advances to her, but in addition he has to listen to his brothers and his father discuss her possible career as a prostitute, and then, to crown it all, observe Ruth strike a hard bargain with them. His principal gesture of defiance against the family who treat him so contemptuously is feeble in the extreme; he steals and eats Lenny's cheese roll. For the rest of the time, he is either silent, or he joins in his own humiliation (as when he explains to Ruth that the family want her to stay behind), or he pretends that everything is quite normal (as when he takes his leave, shaking hands with Lenny and telling Max that it's been wonderful to see him).

However, Teddy's rapid disintegration is totally convincing. From his first appearance with Ruth he is shown to be hesitant and weak, needing to boast to her about taking her to Venice. Just as she dismisses him on that occasion, so the rest of his family remain unimpressed by his wonderful achievements in America. After the argument over the cheese roll, Lenny openly mocks the style of life he imagines Teddy to have in America. Earlier in Act Two, his boasts about his wonderful life at the university evoked no response from his family. This could be because they are envious of his success or because his experience is so remote from their own that they cannot imagine it. Either way his homecoming shows him, ironically, that he no longer has a home to come home to.

Lenny

'I just gave her another belt in the nose and a couple of turns of the boot and sort of left it at that'

Whereas Teddy is passive, unworldly and ineffective, Lenny is vulgar, cruel and mocking. His early interchanges with Max show him to be crude in speech and entirely lacking in respect for his father. However, vulgarity is only one aspect of Lenny's speeches, for he proves himself to be a master of different language and tones. For example, early in Act One, when Max threatens him with his stick, Lenny adopts the voice of the little boy pleading not to be beaten by his cruel father. In this small but revealing example of the struggle for power between father and son, Lenny wins; Max grips his stick but does nothing. (Contrast the incident later in Act One when Max hits Joey, who is not so clever with words as Lenny.) Moments later, Lenny mocks Sam by making what we know (although Sam does not) to be sarcastic enquiries about his day at work.

In his first conversation with Ruth, Lenny seeks to dominate her. He begins by aiming to disorientate her with his talk about his clock; then mocks her in the way he talks about Venice; then tries to surprise her by asking to hold her hand and frighten her by talking about his encounter with a prostitute. At first he succeeds, revealing as he does so a pleasure in violence, especially against women. We notice in his speeches about the prostitute and the old lady that he adopts another tone of voice – one of easy conversation – which makes the horror of what he describes so casually all the more vivid. A little later, having been surprised and put on the defensive by Ruth's open sexuality, he enjoys himself by provoking Max with questions about his own conception. Lenny's ability to use mockery as a form of threat is as apparent here as it was in his conversation with Ruth. On this occasion with Max, Lenny combines mockery of tone with apparent earnestness of enquiry (a device he employs also when talking to Sam about his day at work) which makes him difficult to counter.

Against Lenny's formidable and ruthless skill with language, Teddy has no defence. Whereas Max resorts to vulgarity, Teddy submits. We are given a clear example of this early in Act Two when Lenny questions Teddy on a philosophical topic. Once again, Lenny's gift with words is made clear. He begins by speaking seriously in the manner one would expect of a university professor of philosophy (he takes the words out of Teddy's mouth). But then he soon slips into open mockery by making the highly unlikely claim that his friends in the bar of the Ritz often pass the time discussing such matters. By ridiculing the very language of philosophical debate, he has made it impossible for the topic to be discussed seriously, even if Teddy were capable of doing so.

Lenny's fascination with violence emerges later in Act Two. The account he and Joey give of taking the two girls to the piece of waste ground is obviously intended to shock Teddy. The question is, how true is it? Did it actually happen, or are they inventing it merely to frighten their brother? They tell the story almost like a comic double act, with Lenny prompting Joey from time to time. When Joey seems to forget what Lenny calls the best bit, it is Lenny who continues. If Lenny's stories are true, he is a sadist; if not, he clearly has a diseased imagination.

In the discussions the family have over what to do with Ruth, Lenny shows another aspect of his character – his love of money. Entirely careless about the feelings of others, the only reservation he has about keeping Ruth in the family is the cost. His suggestion that she should become a prostitute shows his debased attitude toward women as well as his willingness to exploit them. It comes as no surprise to learn that he lives off the earnings of a string of prostitutes.

However, clever and immoral though he is, Ruth is his equal. Throughout the play, Lenny has striven for power in the family. At the end, it is Ruth who dominates, although the fact that he is standing watching her implies that he has not succumbed entirely to her power in the way that Joey has, and will continue the struggle.

Max

'I always had a kind heart'

Unpredictable, embittered, foul-mouthed and cruel, Max is a grotesque father figure. It is as though he harbours a grudge against the world which makes him venomous in his relationships. What this grudge might be is something which Pinter never fully explains, thereby making our response to Max all the more dynamic – the more we seek to understand fully why behaves as he does, the more difficult it becomes to do so. It is possible, for instance, that his attitude toward his sons and his brother, and his willingness to debase Ruth, stem from his unhappiness with Jessie. Although nothing reaches the surface until Sam's announcement that MacGregor and Jessie had an affair, there are several dark hints early in the play about them getting on well with each other, and Max himself speaks insultingly of her. Whether Max's ill-nature resulted in her seeking another man, or whether her infidelity (suspected but not admitted by Max) caused him to become embittered, is something we are never told.

Whatever the reason, he seldom misses an opportunity to use his tongue viciously. His brother, each of his sons – especially Teddy – and Ruth are all victims. Why he should be especially abusive to these last two is puzzling, but one possible explanation gives an important insight into his character. Outsiders in Pinter often pose a threat to the status quo. Having left home, married without informing his family and established a style of life different from his brothers and his father, Teddy has become an outsider. When he returns with his wife, it is possible that Max perceives him as a threat to his dominant role in the house. Ruth, too, is an outsider, and also, more significantly, a woman. Max's hatred of women (apparent in the way he spoke of Jessie in Act One) makes her an obvious target. As for Sam, his kindness toward Jessie and the pride he takes in his job make him an irresistible object for Max's cynicism.

Yet for all his self-assertion, Max does not know himself. He tells Ruth early in Act Two that she should live in the present. Yet he himself reconstructs (and probably invents) the past in order to impress others and console himself. There are two particularly good examples of this: he boasts to Lenny about being an expert on horse-racing but it is clear that Lenny does not believe him; and his recreation in Act Two of the simple but happy early years of his marriage is clearly untrue. Like all cynics, Max is sentimental, and the cosy, stereotyped pictures he presents of a devoted wife and smiling, shiny-faced children are fictional.

There are occasions in the play when Max softens, as he does towards the end of Act One and at the start of Act Two. It is hard to know whether these are genuine exhibitions of affection or part of the game he enjoys playing, in which such displays lower the guard of the opposition allowing his next outburst to be all the more shocking.

Although he seeks throughout the play to maintain his position of power, Max loses it in the end, ironically to a woman. He can compete with some success against men, but, as with Jessie, a woman has the power to humiliate a man through sexual betrayal. This is what Max thinks Ruth will do, and suspecting her, yet not wanting to be rejected by her, he ends the play pathetically pleading for a kiss.

Joey

'I've been the whole hog plenty of times'

Joey is the youngest of Max's sons, a man in his middle twenties. He is not as prominent in Act One as he is in Act Two, but certain key aspects of his character become evident early on. Keen to become a successful boxer, Joey practises often at a gymnasium, but Max's remark that he doesn't know how to defend himself or how to attack indicates that while Joey might be very diligent, he lacks any talent. From this, and from the laborious manner in which he speaks, it is possible to deduce also that he is not very intelligent. He contributes only a little more to Act One, refusing to accompany Max to a football match because he has a training session at the gym, and being hit by Max when he does not throw Teddy and Ruth out of the house. There is, however, one important stage direction when Pinter describes Joey watching himself shadow boxing, and then stopping to comb his hair carefully. Put together in this way, they seem to be hinting at another characteristic, vanity.

In Act Two, however, the full unpleasantness of his character becomes clear. He is possessive, brutish, and quick-tempered. When he sees Ruth and Lenny kissing, he eagerly takes her for himself, quite regardless of Teddy's feelings, and later spends two hours with her in bed. So far Pinter has emphasized his selfishness and vanity. Now he enlarges upon Joey's violent nature. His contribution to Lenny's story about the two girls is both moronic and menacing. Reading between the lines, it would seem that he rapes the girl in the car. The unpleasantness of his character is further demonstrated when he behaves childishly over Ruth. Given that the whole situation is disturbing anyway, his remark that he will kill the next person who says that Teddy has had sex with Ruth shows him to be not only violent but petulant, too. In Joey, Pinter has created someone with barely a redeeming quality. Like an animal he is driven by his desires, and can only be controlled by threats or violence.

Sam

'I didn't press myself on people'

Along with Teddy, Sam is a passive character. He takes great pride in his work as a chauffeur, although we come to realize that he is little more than a glorified cab-driver. The sense of importance his job gives him makes him an easy target for the mockery and cynicism of both Lenny and Max. Like Teddy, Sam lacks the ruthlessness to prosper in a family which prides itself so much on self-assertion.

Sam harbours a deep and guilty secret which could, if he chose to use it, provide him with the means of revenging himself on Max: he knows that Jessie and MacGregor had sex with each other in his car as he drove them along. This makes him especially sensitive to Max's crude suggestions that he has been seducing lady customers in the back of the car. A little later, he is anxious to assure Max that although he took Jessie out for drives, he never took advantage of her; he thought too highly of her. What he does not say, at this stage, is that MacGregor did take advantage of her. Sam shows how kind and how weak he is here: he is anxious to put Max's mind at rest in case Max suspects him with Jessie; and he is too kind to use the knowledge he has to humiliate Max in the way Max humiliates him.

It is only towards the end of the play, after he has heard his brother and nephews coldly discussing what to do with Ruth, that he blurts out his secret. It is as though his basic decency can no longer tolerate what is happening in the room, and he uses the only weapon he has to humiliate Max. However, the strain of his outburst is so great that he collapses and cannot contradict Max, who attributes what he has said to a diseased imagination. Decent but ineffectual Sam, like Teddy, will never prosper in a house where only the baser human emotions are on display.

Themes in *The Homecoming*

See general note on themes, p.36.

The Outsider

The threat presented by an outsider is a common theme in Pinter's plays. In *The Homecoming*, there are two outsiders – Teddy and Ruth. Although Teddy is one of the family, he has separated himself by marrying without telling his family, by moving to America, and by being 'successful'. His return home, then, can be seen as posing a threat to the status quo of the family. Lenny, Joey and Max have created a style of life which is not satisfactory but which follows an established pattern; even Sam is part of this pattern. Into this comes Teddy – intelligent, highly educated, inhabiting a world more refined and socially acceptable – who by his very presence is bound to awaken jealousy. As the eldest son, he presents a threat to Max's power in the household, and also to Lenny's position, for in Teddy's absence it is Lenny who is second-in-command.

It is unlikely, of course, that Teddy deliberately means to threaten in this way. But the return of a successful member of the family cannot help but remind the others of the circumstances in which he left them. Teddy assumes that nothing will have changed; he is pleased to find his room left as it was. We note, however, a little later, Lenny's remark that friends of his use it when they are passing. In other words, Lenny is subtly hinting that Teddy's room is no longer exclusively *his*. Later, in Act Two, it is Lenny once more who draws attention to Teddy's ambiguous position in the family. He mentions the empty chair in the circle and reminds Teddy that he is an integral part of the family. Yet the empty chair (if there is one and the entire story is not a lie concocted by Lenny) is as much an accusation of Teddy's betrayal of the family by his departure from them as it is a sign that he is still one of them.

Given that Teddy is now a social and cultural outsider, it is virtually inevitable that the family will seek to demean him, to revenge themselves for his betrayal of them. Teddy assumes that he will return to a home held in some kind of suspended animation from the time he left. He discovers to his cost that instead of being impressed by his success and pleased for him, his family subject him to total sexual, academic and professional humiliation and drive him out. In this they show the same kind of instincts as some animals which, no matter how much they squabble amongst themselves, will always band together to see off an outsider. In this way, Pinter gives an archetypal significance to the action of the play.

The other outsider, Ruth, is more successful. Like all wives, she is apprehensive about first meeting her in-laws. A woman in a house full of men who, Sam apart, dislike women, she seems to be in a particularly weak position. However, as the only woman – and a very attractive one – she uses her most powerful weapon, her sexuality, to ensure she achieves a position of power.

Women and sexuality

Although Ruth is the only woman to appear in the play, several others are mentioned: Jessie, the prostitute Lenny meets at the docks, the old woman with the mangle, and the two girls in the car. With the exception of the old woman, they are all shown to have a sexual dimension, and without exception they are shown to be untrustworthy, unreliable or demanding. Jessie has an affair with MacGregor; the prostitute starts taking liberties with Lenny; the old woman does nothing to help him while he is trying to move her mangle; the two women in the car quickly forget about their escorts; and Ruth not only abandons Teddy but, it seems, uses her sexuality to dominate the others.

With the exception of Sam and Teddy, who are timid, none of the men in the play shows much concern for the happiness of women. Teddy would like Ruth to be happy, but his failure to make her so becomes increasingly evident in her willingness to abandon him. Although he gives the impression that he sees Ruth as a successful woman in her own right, we suspect that he really regards her as an extension of himself and his concerns; she is a good wife and mother. The greatest thrill he can offer her when they return to America is helping him with his lectures.

Max, Lenny and Joey all regard women as treacherous objects who exist to be exploited. Thus Lenny has a group of prostitutes working for him; he and Joey spend evenings cruising in a car looking for likely girls they can either seduce or rape. Women who prove troublesome are treated violently – the prostitute under the bridge, Joey's girl in the car.

Given that women are either extensions of their husbands or sexual objects to be used or abused by men, how are they to survive? In so far as *The Homecoming* offers any answer to this question, it seems to lie with Ruth. As a former photographic model, Ruth, too, was exploited sexually. Her response as a woman to a world in which women are denied individual identity is not to rebel, but to exploit her womanhood for her own benefit. Men like Max, Joey and Lenny like to think that women are submissive and easily managed. Joey in particular exhibits the brutal, possessive nature of men when he insists that he will not share Ruth. It is not that he loves her, but that he sees her as an object which he wants for himself. Ruth lets them believe all this, and then uses her sexuality to devastating effect. The way she offers herself to Lenny on their first meeting, and then her sexually suggestive explanation of the philosophical problem that is troubling Lenny, show her ability to take men by surprise. Having awoken their desire, she briskly dominates the business proceedings when it comes to discussing the conditions on which she will remain with them. The men who had naturally thought they would dominate her find themselves dominated by her. It is not a question of morality, but of survival; not of justice but of power.

Power and survival

This theme is inevitably linked to the previous one, for it is Ruth's determination to survive which makes her seek power. But the entire play, not only Ruth's contribution, is built around the theme of power. In the family, one dominates or is dominated; the choice is as stark as that. To be kind and mild-mannered like Sam is to be vulnerable and open to ridicule. As father and elder brother, Max dominates Joey (even beating him to the ground on one occasion) and Sam, but he does not find it so easy to rule Lenny, his elder son in the absence of Teddy.

In *The Homecoming*, Pinter explores an archetypal phenomenon; that is, the primitive but inevitable contest for power between father and eldest son. In Teddy's absence, this struggle revolves around Max and Lenny. Lenny proves to be a resourceful opponent; Max might raise his stick to him, but he never actually beats him, and once Lenny reduces Max to the feeble response of spitting at him. How must Lenny and Max then feel when another, relatively unknown, opponent enters? An opponent who actually *is* the eldest son? And an opponent who brings into their closed circle an experience of life beyond them. Inevitably, they will seek to drive him out because he is a threat to both of them. It proves to be surprisingly easy, but in seeking to heap the ultimate humiliation on Teddy's head – taking away his woman – they bring about their own downfall. Robbing Teddy of Ruth is the absolute demonstration of their power. What they fail to realize is that Ruth also has entered the game. It is one of the richest thematic ironies in the play that Max loses power not to his eldest son (who proves to be no competition) nor to his second-eldest son, but to a woman he had dismissed as a tart.

Memories, truth and illusions

The past, whether recent or distant, figures largely in the play. Only Joey, the most stupid of all the characters, exists without reference to the past. His most graphic memory is of the time he and Lenny picked up two girls, but even here he needs continual prompting by his more intelligent older brother. As for Sam, the memory of taking Jessie out for drives remains with him still, as does the incident with MacGregor in the back of the car. If Joey is unable to remember the past, Sam cannot forget it, at least this part of it. The guilt he feels for what happened to Jessie, the delight he felt in her company, remain as strong as they ever were. Ruth, too, has one potent memory in the play. Her account of her visits to the house in the country is at once vague but highly suggestive. It comes just after she has alluded to her work as a model before she had all her children. She has only three, and so her use of the word 'all' suggests that she feels trapped in the role of motherhood. The visits to the house recreate a fragment of time when she was free, at least by comparison with her suffocating life with Teddy. Through the hesitant, broken way she speaks of her visits, Pinter displays her great but suppressed emotion. It is as though the recreation in her mind of the memory is at once necessary to her but also painful because it highlights her present unhappiness.

The dividing line between memory and illusion is a fine one in Pinter. The three memories mentioned above are probably true (although we have no way of verifying this), in that they are likely to have happened in the manner in which they are described. But what are we to make of Max's memories of horse-racing and the rosy picture he paints of family life? Or Lenny's stories of the prostitute at the docks, and the old woman, and the story of his interest in philosophy? Or Teddy's description to Ruth of his family being very warm people? Or his accounts of the desirable nature of their life in America? Pinter denies us the means of knowing. What actually is true, what people think is true, and what are downright lies are often difficult to distinguish. This is an intentional device on Pinter's part which he sustains brilliantly in the play, making it at once very realistic (much of what people tell you is difficult to prove absolutely), but also a very distinctive dramatic/theatrical experience in which we can only judge the characters on what we know of them in the play. When we try to use the past to build up a picture of them, we find ourselves having to tread very carefully.

Of all the characters in the play, it is Max and Teddy who seem most to need illusion to comfort them. Even if their memories, long-term in the case of Max, short-term in the case of Teddy, are untrue, they are still important. Their need to create illusions by reinterpreting their experience of life into a rosy acceptable form hints at a bitter disappointment with the nature of their lives, and makes them more interesting and complex figures.

As for Lenny, if his stories are fiction, they are so for a different purpose. He invents not to recreate the past as he wished it had been, but to manipulate the present to his own advantage. With Ruth, it is to frighten her with stories of his violence to women; with Teddy it is to ridicule him.

Language and comedy

The Homecoming is a very funny play, but Pinter creates the comedy out of material which surprises or disgusts us: for example, the abusive language the family use to each other which clearly shows mutual hatred; the mockery of the eldest son by his father and brothers; the violent stories; the treatment of Teddy's wife; Ruth's businesslike manner as she discusses her new career as a prostitute.

Most obviously, laughter comes from the insults which are hurled round, but if Pinter relied principally on this device the play would be little better than a tired television sit-com. However, he uses language in a dazzling variety of ways to achieve a rich comic texture. He is not above exploiting the old technique of 'the sting in the tail', as he does in Act One when Sam heaps insult upon insult on MacGregor and concludes by observing that he was a good friend of Max, thus insulting Max as well; or when Max himself first speaks well of Jessie and immediately says how looking at her made him sick.

More in Pinter's line is the use of everyday words and phrases in such a way that they are at once comic and unsettling. There is, for instance, the repetition of phrases like going 'the whole hog' or 'the gravy', so that they increase in vulgarity and comic effect the more they are used. Joey's attempt to find the opposite of the phrase 'going the whole hog' always raises a laugh in the theatre because the best he can come up with is 'not going any hog'. Pinter thereby underlines his brutal stupidity.

Typical of Pinter, too, is the way in which he can create a comedy of menace by having a character begin a story in an ordinary conversational manner and switch abruptly to the language of violence as though there is no difference between the two. For instance, when Lenny tells Ruth the story of the prostitute he met, he begins with some amusingly incorrect details about what the sailors were doing; then he uses rather prim, polite language ('a lady', 'a certain proposal', 'taking liberties') to describe the actual encounter, before talking about murdering her as if it were an event of small consequence. A little later, in the story of the old lady, we have the same kind of gruesome detail given in an easy, conversational manner.

Instead of beating her up properly, he says, he merely punched her once in the stomach and jumped on a bus outside, as though it were the most natural thing in the world. The juxtaposition of the ordinary event like jumping on a bus alongside the monstrousness of assaulting an old woman generate both the comedy and the horror.

More generally, there is the unpleasant and disturbing comic irony of two members of the family discussing the idea of putting another family member on the streets. The blasé way in which they do this produces an effect of comic horror, but this is topped when the woman herself actually agrees, in the presence of her husband, to become a prostitute. The comedy here resides not only in the business-like nature of the language when applied to something so obscene, but in the grotesque nature of the situation itself.

The comedy of *The Homecoming* is not the kind which brings a warm, consoling glow. Our laughter is uneasy because it is aroused by characters who are immoral, violent and selfish. Whenever we indulge ourselves in laughter, we have to stop and consider what we are laughing at, and the answer often tells us something rather unpleasant about ourselves.

Structure

Built around the members of one family, and with the action taking place in one room. *The Homecoming* presents a situation which is at once natural in its setting and bizarre in its action. The structure takes the form of a series of ironic reversals. For instance, Teddy, the philosopher, is shown up by his younger brother in a discussion about philosophy; Joey, the boxer, is almost felled by a blow from his aged father; Sam, the gentle brother, blurts out the truth about Jessie and Mac; Ruth, who in her first scene speaks of her children, abandons them by the end.

This pattern of ironic reversal is given its greatest significance in Ruth, however. In fact, one could say that the whole play is structured around the idea of the men, with the exception of Sam, treating Ruth either patronizingly, abusively or menacingly and ending up defeated or, in the case of Lenny, strongly challenged by her. As this pattern develops, each reversal is more outrageous than the last. We can see this pattern, for example, in her first scene (and subsequently) with Teddy, her first scene with Lenny, the way in which she allows Joey to fondle her and take her to bed but stops him short of having sex with her, the way in which, after all Max's abuse, she renders him abject at the end, and the way in which instead of allowing herself to be the victim of her in-laws' greed and lust, she drives them into making concessions.

General questions on *The Homecoming*

1 By careful reference to the play, show how power is one of the principal ideas presented.

Suggested notes for essay answer:
a) Max's behaviour to other members of the family; (b) the way Lenny treats Max, Ruth and Teddy; c) Ruth's actions. Look closely at the different ways in which power is sought and achieved: by physical violence, by direct verbal threat, by suggestion and innuendo – as when Lenny tries to frighten Ruth with his stories of the prostitute and the old lady – and, with Ruth, by the use of physical attractiveness. Close reference to particular examples is necessary to illustrate the various tactics employed. Consider, too, the irony in the treatment of this theme: Joey, the strongest and youngest, is actually the weakest; Ruth, who appears the weakest and most vulnerable, is actually the strongest. Mention also the function of Teddy and Sam who are dominated. Within the family one cannot choose to be neutral; one either rules or is ruled. There is a perpetual struggle to maintain one's position in the pecking order. Sam's general placidity rather than being respected, is mocked.

2 'Comedy of menace'. How accurate a description of *The Homecoming* is this?

3 Discuss Pinter's presentation of the women who are mentioned in the play but who do not appear. What do they contribute to the play's dramatic effect?

4 Would you agree that Ruth is the most important character in the play?

5 What do either Sam or Joey contribute to the play?

6 What, if anything, does the play gain by being set in one room?

7 What do you learn about the characters from the dreams, memories and illusions they have?

8 If you were asked to say what you thought were the most distinctive features of *The Homecoming*, how would you answer?

9 In what ways would you say that *The Homecoming* can be called realistic?

10 'We shouldn't like Lenny, but most of us have a grudging regard for him.' Would you agree?

11 Do you have any sympathy for Teddy?

12 How does the portrayal of the family in *The Homecoming* differ from a family in any other book you have read?

13 Compare and contrast *The Homecoming* with any other book you have read which includes comedy and/or violence.

14 Write about any other book in which there is a surprise ending. How does the writer manage to take you by surprise?

15 Examine the presentation of marriage in any other book you have read.

Further reading list

Here are some more plays by Pinter which are worth reading.

The Room and *The Dumb Waiter*, Eyre Methuen 1966

Old Times, Eyre Methuen, 1972

The Collection, Eyre Methuen, 1975

A Slight Ache and other plays, Eyre Methuen, 1975

Tea Party and other plays, Eyre Methuen, 1975

No Man's Land, Eyre Methuen, 1976

Betrayal, Eyre Methuen, 1980

The Hothouse, Eyre Methuen, 1982

One for the Road, Eyre Methuen, 1985

Here are some critical works on Pinter you might find helpful.

Harold Pinter, Harold Dukore, Macmillan Educational 1988

Pinter: The Playwright, Martin Esslin, Methuen, 1982

Harold Pinter: Twentieth-Century Views, Arthur Ganz (ed), Prentice Hall, 1972.